THE MARKETING PLAN HANDBOOK

ALEXANDER CHERNEV

Kellogg School of Management

Northwestern University

FIFTH EDITION

D1262464

No part of this publication may be recorded, stored in a retrieval system, or transmitted in any form or by any means electronic, mechanical, photocopying, recording, scanning, or otherwise, except as permitted under Section 107 or 108 of the United States Copyright Act, without the prior written permission of the publisher. Requests to the publisher for permission should be addressed to Cerebellum Press, Inc., at permissions@cerebellumpress.com.

While the publisher and the author have used their best efforts in preparing this book, they make no representations or warranties with respect to the accuracy or completeness of the contents of this book and specifically disclaim any implied warranties of merchantability or fitness for a particular purpose. The advice and strategies contained herein may not be suitable for your situation. Neither the publisher nor the author shall be liable for any loss of profit or any other commercial damages, including but not limited to special, incidental, consequential, or other damages.

The Marketing Plan Handbook

Fifth Edition | January 2018

ISBN: 978-1-936572-55-7 (Paperback)

ISBN: 978-1-936572-56-4 (Hardcover)

Copyright © 2009–2018 by Alexander Chernev

www.CHERNEV.com

Published by Cerebellum Press, USA

TABLE OF CONTENTS

Alexander Chernev is a professor of marketing at the Kellogg School of Management, Northwestern University. He holds a PhD in psychology and a second PhD in business administration from Duke University.

Dr. Chernev has written numerous articles focused on business strategy, brand management, consumer behavior, and marketing planning. His research has been published in the leading marketing journals and has been frequently quoted in the business and popular press, including *The Wall Street Journal, Financial Times, The New York Times, The Washington Post, Harvard Business Review, Scientific American, Associated Press, Forbes,* and *Business Week.* He was ranked among the top ten most prolific scholars in the leading marketing journals by the *Journal of Marketing* and among the top five marketing faculty in the area of consumer behavior by a global survey of marketing faculty published by the *Journal of Marketing Education.*

Dr. Chernev's books — *Strategic Marketing Management, Strategic Brand Management, The Marketing Plan Handbook,* and *The Business Model: How to Develop New Products, Create Market Value, and Make the Competition Irrelevant* — have been translated into multiple languages and are used in top business schools and by marketing executives around the world. He serves as an area editor for the *Journal of Marketing* and is on the editorial boards of leading research journals, including the *Journal of Marketing Research, Journal of Consumer Research, Journal of Consumer Psychology, Journal of the Academy of Marketing Science,* and *Journal of Marketing Behavior.*

Dr. Chernev teaches marketing strategy, brand management, and behavioral decision theory in MBA, PhD, and executive education programs at the Kellogg School of Management. He has also taught in executive programs at INSEAD in France and Singapore, at the Institute for Management Development (IMD) in Switzerland, and at Hong Kong University of Science and Technology. He has received numerous teaching awards, including the Chairs' Core Course Teaching Award, Kellogg Faculty Impact Award, and the Top Professor Award from the Kellogg Executive MBA Program, which he has received nine times.

In addition to research and teaching, Dr. Chernev is an Academic Trustee of the *Marketing Science Institute* and advises companies around the world on issues of marketing strategy, brand management, consumer behavior, pricing, strategic planning, and new product development. He has worked with Fortune 500 companies on ways to reinvent their business models, develop new products, and gain competitive advantage. He is an early-stage investor and has helped multiple startups to uncover market opportunities, craft their business models, and implement their market strategies.

ACKNOWLEDGMENTS

This book has benefited from the wisdom of many of my current and former colleagues at the Kellogg School of Management at Northwestern University: Nidhi Agrawal, Eric Anderson, Jim Anderson, Robert Blattberg, Ulf Böckenholt, Anand Bodapati, Miguel Brendl, Bobby Calder, Tim Calkins, Gregory Carpenter, Moran Cerf, Yuxin Chen, Anne Coughlan, Patrick Duparcq, David Gal, Kelly Goldsmith, Kent Grayson, Sachin Gupta, Karsten Hansen, Julie Hennessy, Dawn Iacobucci, Dipak Jain, Robert Kozinets, Aparna Labroo, Lakshman Krishnamurthi, Eric Leininger, Angela Lee, Sidney Levy, Michal Maimaran, Prashant Malaviya, Eyal Maoz, Blake McShane, Vikas Mittal, Vincent Nijs, Christie Nordhielm, Mary Pearlman, Yi Qian, Neal Roese, Derek Rucker, Mohan Sawhney, John Sherry, Jr., Louis Stern, Brian Sternthal, Rima Touré-Tillery, Anna Tuchman, Alice Tybout, Rick Wilson, Song Yao, Philip Zerrillo, Florian Zettelmeyer, and Andris Zoltners.

I would like to thank Andrea Bonezzi (New York University), Aaron Brough (Utah State University), Pierre Chandon (INSEAD), Akif Irfan (Goldman Sachs), Mathew Isaac (Seattle University), Ryan Hamilton (Emory University), Ajay Kohli (Georgia Institute of Technology), and Jaya Sah (Goldman Sachs) for their valuable comments.

I owe a considerable debt of gratitude to Philip Kotler, one of the leading thinkers in the field of marketing, who through his insightful writings sparked my interest in marketing. I am also indebted to Jim Bettman, Julie Edell Britton, Joel Huber, John Lynch, John Payne, and Rick Staelin at the Fuqua School of Business at Duke University for their advice and support at the outset of my academic career.

PREFACE

The Marketing Plan Handbook presents a streamlined approach to writing succinct and meaningful marketing plans. By offering a comprehensive, step-by-step method to crafting a strategically viable marketing plan, this book provides the relevant information in a concise and straight-to-the-point manner. It outlines the basic principles of writing a marketing plan and presents an overarching framework that encompasses the plan's essential components.

A distinct characteristic of this book is its emphasis on marketing as a value-creation process. Because it incorporates the three aspects of value management—managing customer value, managing collaborator value, and managing company value—the marketing plan outlined in this book is relevant not only for business-to-consumer scenarios but for business-to-business scenarios as well. This integration of business-to-consumer and business-to-business planning into a single framework is essential for ensuring success in today's networked marketplace.

The marketing plan outlined in this book builds on the view of marketing as a central business discipline that defines the key aspects of a company's business model. This view of marketing is reflected in the book's cross-functional approach to strategic business planning. The Marketing Plan Handbook offers an integrative approach to writing a marketing plan that incorporates the relevant technological, financial, organizational, and operational aspects of the business. This approach leads to a marketing plan that is pertinent not only for marketers but for the entire organization.

The Marketing Plan Handbook can benefit managers in all types of organizations. For startups and companies considering bringing new products to the market, this book outlines a process for developing a marketing plan to launch a new offering. For established companies with existing portfolios of products, this book presents a structured approach to developing an action plan to manage their offerings and product lines. Whether it is applied to a small business seeking to formalize the planning process, a startup seeking venture-capital financing, a fast-growth company considering an initial public offering, or a large multinational corporation, the framework outlined in this book can help streamline the marketing planning process and translate it into an actionable strategic document that informs business decisions and helps avoid costly missteps.

The Marketing Plan Handbook is designed for managers who are already familiar with the basics of strategic marketing management and seek to develop meaningful, action-oriented marketing plans that generate tangible results. Readers interested in refreshing their knowledge of strategic analysis and planning are encouraged to consult more comprehensive marketing textbooks, such as Marketing Management by Philip Kotler and Kevin Keller and Strategic Marketing Management by Alexander Chernev.

PART ONE

THE MARKETING PLAN

INTRODUCTION

The marketing plan is a written document that defines a company's goals, delineates a course of action aimed at achieving these goals, and provides guidelines for evaluating the progress toward these goals. The success of the marketing plan depends on its ability to apply marketing theories and frameworks to the specific problems faced by the organization. Accordingly, the first part of this book presents an overview of the key marketing concepts involved in developing a marketing plan. In particular, this part comprises three chapters:

Chapter 1 discusses the role of the marketing plan as a strategic business document, focusing on issues such as the purpose of the marketing plan; the key principles and entities involved in writing a marketing plan; the target audience for the marketing plan; the focus, length, and time horizon of the marketing plan; and the frequency of updating the marketing plan.

Chapter 2 offers a big-picture overview of the marketing fundamentals, focusing on the two key components of a company's value-creation model: strategy and tactics. A company's strategy and tactics are discussed in the context of the market value principle, which defines the primary goal of an offering as creating superior value for target customers and the company's collaborators in a way that enables the company to reach its goals. The strategy and tactics are the cornerstone of the G-STIC framework that is the backbone of marketing planning.

Chapter 3 builds on the G-STIC framework to outline the organization of the marketing plan. It delineates the key components of the marketing plan—executive summary, situation overview, goal, strategy, tactics, implementation, control, and exhibits—and presents the key principles in developing each individual component.

These three chapters establish the purpose, the logic, and the structure of the marketing plan and are followed by specific examples laid out in Part Two of this book.

Chapter One

The Marketing Plan
as a Business Document

*A good deal of corporate planning is like a ritual rain dance; it has
no effect on the weather that follows. Moreover, much of the advice
and instruction is directed at improving the dancing, not the weather.*

— James Brian Quinn
Professor of Management,
Dartmouth University

The marketing plan is a written document that identifies a specific goal and outlines a course of action to achieve this goal. It can concern a particular offering, a product line, or the entire company. The key principles of developing a viable marketing plan are the focus of this chapter.

Overview

Writing a marketing plan is often confused with strategic planning, partially because strategic planning is frequently driven by the need to generate a marketing plan. Strategic planning and writing a marketing plan are two distinct activities. Strategic planning is the process of identifying a goal and developing a course of action to achieve this goal. A marketing plan puts into writing an already identified goal and the decided-on course of action. The marketing plan is the tangible outcome of a company's strategic planning process.

Because marketing covers only one aspect of a company's business activities, the marketing plan is narrower in scope than the business plan. In addition to focusing on the marketing aspect of the company's activities, the business plan addresses financial, operations, human resource, and technological aspects. The marketing plan may include a brief overview of other aspects of the company's business processes, but only to the extent they are related to the marketing plan.

In addition to developing an overall marketing plan, companies often develop more specialized plans. Such plans include a product development plan, service management plan, brand management plan, sales plan, promotion plan, communication plan, and distribution plan. Some of these plans can, in turn, comprise even more specific plans. For example, a company's communication plan might comprise a series of activity-specific plans, such as an advertising plan, public relations plan, mobile communication plan, and social media plan. The ultimate success of each of these individual plans depends on the degree to which they are consistent with the overall marketing plan.

The Purpose of a Marketing Plan

The primary purpose of a marketing plan is to clearly articulate the company's goal and the desired course of action and effectively communicate them to the relevant parties: employees, collaborators, and stakeholders. In particular, the marketing plan can serve the following functions:

- **Delineate the proposed course of action.** Because marketing plans are written documents, they often force managers to be specific in their analysis and articulate in greater detail different aspects of the proposed action. This greater level of detail enables the marketing plan to serve as a guide for tactical decisions such as product development, service management, branding, pricing, sales promotions, communication, and distribution. In addition to articulating the proposed course of action, the marketing plan can identify the composition of the team managing the offering and the allocation of responsibilities among individual members of the team.

- **Inform relevant stakeholders of the goal and proposed course of action.** By providing uniform information to all stakeholders, the marketing plan helps ensure that all relevant parties are on the same page with respect to the specifics of the offering. Because most offerings are developed, promoted, and distributed in collaboration with other entities, having a common understanding of the primary goal and the proposed course of action to achieve that goal is essential for an offering's success.

- **"Sell" the proposed goal and course of action.** An important and often overlooked function of the marketing plan is to persuade the relevant stakeholders of the viability of the set goal and the identified course of action. The marketing plan can be the key factor in senior management's decision to proceed with the proposed action and the primary driver of collaborators' decision to support the company's offering.

The overarching goal of the marketing plan is to inform relevant stakeholders about the company's action plan and ensure that their actions are consistent with the company's ultimate goal.

Three Key Principles in Developing a Marketing Plan

Most marketing plans suffer from a common problem. Rather than fulfilling their vital mission of steering company actions to attain a stated goal, they are frequently written merely to fulfill the requirement of having a document filed in the company archives. As a result, marketing plans often substitute exhaustive analyses of marginally relevant issues and laundry lists of activities for a meaningful course of action. The lack of internal logic and cohesiveness often leads to haphazard actions that fall far short of helping the company achieve its strategic goals.

To be effective, the marketing plan must outline a sound goal and a viable action plan to achieve this goal, and communicate this strategy to the target audience. Specifically, the marketing plan must be *actionable, clear,* and *succinct.*

- **Actionable.** The marketing plan should delineate a course of action aimed at achieving the company's goal. The proposed course of action typically involves developing or modifying one or more of the attributes of the company's offering: product, service, brand, price, incentives, communication, and distribution. Accordingly, the marketing plan must define the proposed actions related to the company's offering, the time frame for implementing these actions, and the entities responsible for implementing them.

- **Clear.** A key goal of the marketing plan is to inform the relevant stakeholders about a company's action plan and convince them of the viability of the proposed action. Therefore, the marketing plan should clearly articulate the goal the company aims to achieve and delineate the essence of the proposed action. Because the marketing plan contains information concerning different aspects of the proposed action — its goal, strategy, tactics, implementation, and metrics for evaluating its performance — this information must be presented in a systematic manner that underscores the logic of the proposed course of action. The clarity of a manager's thought process is reflected in the organization of the marketing plan. Streamlined marketing plans indicate streamlined business thinking.

- **Succinct.** Most marketing plans suffer from a common problem: They are unnecessarily long and filled with marginally relevant information. Managers developing such plans are often driven by the misguided notion that the length of the plan reflects the depth of thinking about the proposed course of action and, hence, longer marketing plans are inherently more viable than shorter ones. While it is true that the length of the marketing plan is sometimes used as an indicator of broader analysis and deeper thinking, more managers have come to realize that shorter plans are often better than longer ones. When it comes to writing marketing plans, it is often the case that *less is more.*

Following the above three principles — actionability, clarity, and conciseness — can help the company ensure that its marketing plan will effectively guide its market actions and will enable the company to reach its strategic goals.

Who Is Involved in Developing the Marketing Plan

Because marketing cuts across different types of company activities, the development and the implementation of the marketing plan typically is not done by a single entity. Instead, the marketing plan is created by soliciting input from multiple entities that play different roles: *the project leader, the management team, influencers,* and *gatekeepers.*

- **Project leader** is the person in charge of managing the offering and the planning process. The project leader is also ultimately responsible for implementing the marketing plan and for producing a desirable outcome.

- **Management team** are individuals working with the project leader to develop and manage the offering. The management team is often cross-functional, comprising experts from different areas such as research and development, information technology, operations, finance, marketing, purchasing, and the sales force.

- **Influencers** are entities outside the management team that have an impact on the development of the marketing plan by sharing their preferences and providing recommendations.

- **Gatekeepers** are entities that must approve the plan before it is put into action. For example, an offering's pricing policy, exclusivity agreements, and the content of communication campaigns often need to be approved by a company's legal department before the marketing plan can be put into action.

The goal of the project leader is to gather insights and get buy-in from the relevant entities — the management team, influencers, and gatekeepers — to ensure not only that the marketing plan is viable but also that it will be supported by the key stakeholders.

The Target Audience

To develop a meaningful plan, managers need to know their audience. Most marketing plans target four major audiences: *employees, collaborators, stakeholders,* and *senior management.*

- **Employees.** Often viewed as the primary target audience for the marketing plan, company employees comprise two different groups: members of the team managing the offering and company employees not directly involved in the offering. For the members of the team in charge of the offering, the marketing plan provides information about the specifics of the proposed action plan and outlines the particular actions to be taken, their sequence, and the time frame. For employees not directly involved with the offering, the marketing plan provides an overview of the goals and the key aspects of the proposed course of action.

- **Collaborators.** An important function of the marketing plan is to inform and bring on board all external entities whose collaboration is essential for implementing the plan. These entities include product development partners, communication (e.g., advertising and public relations) agencies, suppliers, distributors (e.g., wholesalers and retailers), sales force, and marketing research companies. Ensuring that these collaborators are aware of the key aspects of the company's goal, strategy, and tactics is an essential precondition for the offering's success.

- **Stakeholders.** The success of a company's offering also depends on the support from the company's stakeholders. These stakeholders include entities with a direct or indirect financial interest in the company (e.g., shareholders, bondholders, and creditors), as well as entities that have a more general interest in the company's actions (e.g., regulatory agencies, trade organizations, and consumer activist groups). The marketing plan should inform these stakeholders about the company's proposed actions to ensure their approval and support.

- **Senior management.** Senior management must give the final approval of the plan before it is put into action. Senior management can involve company employees (e.g., the chief marketing officer or the chief executive officer) or a governing entity (e.g., the board of directors). Unlike the gatekeepers, whose primary function is to ensure that a specific aspect of the plan conforms to a set of policies (e.g., legal regulations, technical specifications, or financial requirements), senior management has the power (and the responsibility) to give the "go ahead" to the marketing plan as a whole.

Because it targets a broad audience with different levels of functional expertise and different levels of involvement, the marketing plan must be written in a way that is understandable, informative, and meaningful to each audience segment.

The Length of the Marketing Plan

The length of the marketing plan depends on the specifics of the underlying offering. Plans for more complex, broad-in-scope offerings involving multiple collaborators operating in a multifaceted economic, sociocultural, regulatory, technological, and physical context tend to be longer than plans for relatively simple offerings.

The length of the plan is also a function of a variety of extrinsic factors unrelated to the specific offering. For example, many companies have a legacy of creating marketing plans of a certain length, to which managers are expected to adhere. Even in the absence of a preconceived expectation of the plan's length, there is a common belief that longer plans reflect a more thorough analysis and, therefore, are inherently superior to plans that are less voluminous. Despite its intuitive appeal, this belief is often misguided. Longer plans frequently end up being simply a compilation of different reports and can lack a clear outline of the proposed course of action, its goal, and rationale. Moreover, unlike shorter plans, in which the lack of logic is transparent to the reader, longer plans make it easier to hide obscure reasoning.

The preference for longer plans is also heightened by the belief that the length of the plan reflects the amount of effort invested in its development. Although popular, this belief tends to be incorrect. Creating a short and meaningful plan often takes more thought, effort, and time than generating a multipage compilation of a series of unrelated reports.

The development of a marketing plan involves separating the need-to-know information from the nice-to-know information. *Need-to-know* information is crucial for the successful development and implementation of a particular course of action. As suggested by its name, need-to-know information is the knowledge managers must have in order to make an informed decision. In contrast, *nice-to-know* information is tangential to the decision at hand and is not essential for deciding on a particular course of action. Nice-to-know information is potentially interesting but ultimately not actionable and, therefore, unnecessary.

Need-to-know information typically can be acted on; that is, the nature of the information is likely to determine the subsequent course of action. In contrast, nice-to-know information is not directly related to the decision at hand and, hence, is rarely actionable. To illustrate, managers often order multiple research surveys, following the popular view that more data are always better. Yet very few of those managers end up using all the data they acquire. When reports arrive, managers browse the data, comment that "this is a really nice report," and then promptly shelve it. The next time managers touch this report is to trash it to free up space for yet another report containing nice-to-know information.

Another relevant consideration is how much data to include in the marketing plan. Managers tend to be preoccupied with data for several reasons. First, in many organizations there is a legacy of acquiring a large number of unrelated reports on the off chance that they contain useful information. Furthermore, with the advancement of online supply-chain management and e-commerce, many companies have accumulated large amounts of data that could offer potentially valuable insights on the strengths and weaknesses of their business models. Collecting data consistent with a given course of action also helps quantify the logic of the proposed course of action as well as prepare a defense in case of failure. All these reasons notwithstanding, simply gathering more data does not necessarily make for a more effective marketing plan. To be effective, the marketing plan should include only need-to-know information that is directly relevant to the presented analysis and the proposed course of action.

The Planning Horizon

Marketing plans vary in their time horizon: Some plans have a long-term focus, whereas others aim to achieve short-term goals. Long-term plans provide an overall strategic direction and tend to be more general in nature. In contrast, short-term plans are more specific and provide guidance for the day-to-day activities of the marketing team managing the offering. Typical long-term plans could have a three- to five-year horizon, whereas short-term plans have a time frame of a week, month, or quarter.

The time horizon of the marketing plan depends on a variety of factors. One of the key factors is the degree of uncertainty associated with a particular offering. Offerings that are new to the company and/or operate in rapidly evolving industries tend to have plans with a relatively shorter time horizon, whereas established offerings in mature industries tend to have plans with a relatively longer time horizon. Because the presence of strategic uncertainty makes the development of detailed plans virtually impossible, long-term marketing plans tend to be more strategic in nature.

Long-term marketing plans are important because they are more likely to recognize the impact of activities such as brand building, enhancements in an offering's performance on attributes such as reliability and durability, and customer-service improvements—all of which have a delayed impact on the offering's performance. Without a long-term plan, managers are likely to focus their attentions only on activities that have immediate impact. For example, a manager whose performance is measured on a quarterly basis is likely to engage in activities that lead to short-term results such as sales promotions, and less likely to invest in activities such as brand building that have a long-term payoff.

Updating the Marketing Plan

Once developed, marketing plans need updating in order to remain relevant. *Plans are of little importance, but planning is essential*, wrote British politician and military strategist Winston Churchill, highlighting the importance of flexibility in strategic planning. There are two common reasons to consider updating the marketing plan: *performance gaps* reflecting a discrepancy between the company's desired and actual performance and *changes in the target market*.

Closing Performance Gaps

Performance gaps involve a discrepancy between a company's desired and actual performance on a key metric such as net income, profit margins, and sales revenues. Performance gaps typically stem from three main sources: *inaccurate information* about the target market, including unforeseen market changes, *logic flaws* in the marketing plan, and *implementation errors* that involve poor execution of a viable marketing plan.

- **Inaccurate information.** When developing the marketing plan, managers rarely have all the necessary information at their fingertips. It is often the case that, despite the voluminous amount of information accumulated, certain strategically important pieces of information—competitive intelligence, technological developments, and future government regulations—are not readily available. As a result, managers must fill in the information gaps by making certain assumptions. Updating the plan to reduce the uncertainty contained in such assumptions and increasing the accuracy of the information that serves as the basis for the company's marketing plan can bolster the plan's effectiveness.

- **Logic flaws.** Another common source of performance gaps is the presence of logic flaws in the design of the marketing plan. For example, the proposed strategy might be inconsistent with the set goal, whereby an otherwise viable strategy might not produce desired results. In the same vein, the offering's tactics might be inconsistent with the desired strategy, whereby product attributes might not create value for target customers, the price might be too high, and/or communication and distribution channels might be inadequate. The presence of logic flaws in the marketing plan necessitates revising the plan to eliminate any logical inconsistencies in the ways the company aims to create market value.

- **Implementation errors.** Performance gaps can also stem from implementation errors involving poor execution of an otherwise viable marketing plan. This type of error occurs because managers do not adhere to the actions prescribed by the marketing plan (e.g., they are unfamiliar with the plan), because their intuition based (erroneously) on prior experience contradicts the proposed course of action, or due to a lack of discipline (often imbued in a company's culture) to systematically implement the agreed-on marketing plan. The presence of implementation errors calls for revising the process of managing the offering and/or reevaluating the relevant personnel.

Responding to Market Changes

Market changes involve changes in one or more of the Five Cs—the five factors that define the market in which the company operates: (1) changes in target customers' demographics, buying power, needs, and preferences; (2) changes in the competitive environment, such as a new competitive entry, price cuts, launch of an aggressive advertising campaign, and/or expanded distribution; (3) changes in the collaborator environment, such as a threat of backward integration from the distribution channel, increased trade margins, and consolidation among retailers; (4) changes in the company, such as the acquisition or loss of strategic assets and competencies; and (5) changes in the market context, such as an economic recession, the development of a new technology, and new legal regulations.

To illustrate, in response to the change in the needs and preferences of its *customers*, many fast-food restaurants, including McDonald's, redefined their offerings to include healthier options. To respond to the new type of *competition* from online retailers, many traditional brick-and-mortar retailers—such as Walmart, Macy's, and Best Buy—redefined their business models and become multichannel retailers. In the same vein, many manufacturers had to extend their product lines to include lower tier offerings in response to their *collaborators'* (retailers) widespread adoption of private labels. The development or acquisition of *company* assets, such as patents and proprietary technologies, can call for redefining the underlying business models in virtually any industry. Finally, changes in *context*, such as the ubiquity of mobile communication, e-commerce, and social media, have disrupted the extant value-creation processes, forcing companies to redefine their business models.

Updating a marketing plan involves modifying the company's current course of action and can include the need to reevaluate the current goal, redesign the existing strategy (identify new target markets, and/or modify the overall value proposition of the offering for customers, collaborators, and the company), change the tactics (improve the product, enhance the service, reposition the brand, modify the price, introduce new incentives, streamline communication, and introduce new channels of distribution), streamline the implementation, and develop alternative controls. The key principle in updating the action plan is that the changes in the plan should address the inefficiencies in the existing marketing plan while responding to market changes.

To succeed, the ways in which a company creates market value must evolve with the changes in the market in which it operates. Companies that fail to adapt their business models and market plans to reflect the new market reality tend to fade away, their businesses engulfed by companies with superior business models better equipped to create market value. According to Charles Darwin, *It is not the strongest of the species that survives, nor the most intelligent, but the one most responsive to change.* The key to market success is not only generating a viable market plan but also honing the ability to adapt this plan to changes in the marketplace.

ADDITIONAL READINGS

Chernev, Alexander (2018), *Strategic Marketing Management* (9th ed.). Chicago, IL: Cerebellum Press.

Calkins, Tim (2012), *Breakthrough Marketing Plans: How to Stop Wasting Time and Start Driving Growth* (2nd ed.). New York, NY: Palgrave Macmillan.

Kotler, Philip and Kevin Lane Keller (2015), *Marketing Management* (15th ed.). Upper Saddle River, NJ: Prentice Hall.

CHAPTER TWO

THE FRAMEWORK FOR MARKETING PLANNING

Vision without action is a daydream.
Action without vision is a nightmare.
—Japanese proverb

A company's success is defined by its ability to create market value. To create value, a company must clearly identify the target market in which it will compete; develop a meaningful value proposition for its target customers, collaborators, and the company stakeholders; and design an offering that will deliver this value proposition to the target market. These activities define the two key components of a company's business model: strategy and tactics. The strategy defines the target market and the value the company aims to create in this market. The tactics, on the other hand, define the attributes of the offering that is being exchanged in the market. The key aspects of defining an offering's strategy and tactics and the development of a value-driven action plan are the focus of this chapter.[1]

Marketing Strategy: Identifying the Target Market

The target market is the market in which a company aims to create and capture value. It is defined by five factors: *customers* whose needs the company aims to fulfill, *competitors* that aim to fulfill the same needs of the same target customers, *collaborators* that work with the company to fulfill customers' needs, the *company* managing the offering, and the *context* in which the company operates.

The five market factors are often referred to as the *Five Cs,* and the resulting framework is referred to as the *5-C framework*. The 5-C framework can be visually represented by a set of concentric ellipses, with target customers in the center; collaborators, competitors, and the company in the middle; and the context on the outside (Figure 1). The central placement of target customers reflects their defining role in the market; the other three entities—the company, its collaborators, and its competitors—aim to create value for these customers. The context is the outer layer because it defines the environment in which customers, the company, its collaborators, and its competitors operate.

Figure 1. Identifying the Target Market: The 5-C Framework

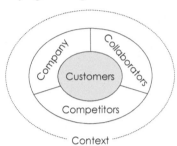

The Five Cs and the relationships among them are discussed in more detail in the following sections.

Target Customers

Target customers are the entities (individuals or organizations) whose needs the company aims to fulfill. In business-to-consumer markets, target customers are the individuals who are typically the end users of the company's offerings. In business-to-business markets, target customers are other businesses that use the company's offerings. Target customers are defined by two factors: *needs* and *profile*.

- Customer needs reflect the specific problem(s) faced by customers that the company aims to address. Customer needs determine the benefits that customers expect to receive from the company's offering. Although of critical importance to the company's ability to create customer value, customer needs are not readily observable and are often inferred from the customer profile.

- Customer profile reflects customers' observable characteristics: *demographics* such as age, gender, income, occupation, education, religion, ethnicity, nationality, employment, geographic location, social class, household size, family life cycle, interests, and hobbies; and *behavior* such as shopping habits, purchase frequency, purchase quantity, price sensitivity, sensitivity to promotional activities, loyalty, and social and leisure activities.

Both factors—needs and profile—are important in defining target customers. Customer needs determine the value the company must create for these customers, and the customer profile identifies effective and cost-efficient ways in which the company can reach customers with these needs to communicate and deliver its offering.

For example, Starbucks fulfills customers' need for a place between home and work where they can enjoy indulgent coffee drinks handcrafted to their personal taste, relax, and socialize. Customers with these needs have different profiles: Most are adult urbanites aged 25 to 40 with relatively high incomes, professional careers, and a sense of social responsibility; the second-largest customer segment is young adults aged 16 to 24, many of whom are college students or young professionals.

The choice of target customers determines all other aspects of the market: the scope of the competition, potential collaborators, company resources necessary to fulfill customer needs, and the context in which the company will create market value. A change in target customers typically leads to a change in competitors and collaborators, requires different company resources, and is influenced by different context factors. Because of its strategic importance, choosing the right target customers is the key to building a successful business model.

Competitors

Competitors are entities that aim to fulfill the same need of the same customers as the company does. Competitors are defined relative to customer needs, not merely based on the industry within which they operate. For example, digital camera manufacturers not only compete with one another; they also compete with the manufacturers of smartphones because both digital cameras and smartphones can fulfill the same customer need of capturing a moment in time.

For example, Starbucks competes with other chain stores offering drip and espresso-based coffee drinks, including Dunkin' Donuts, McDonald's, Costa Coffee, and Peet's Coffee. It also competes with boutique coffee shops offering handcrafted coffee drinks. In addition, Starbucks competes with offerings from the likes of Nespresso and Keurig, whose capsule-based technology enables consumers to easily make drip and espresso coffee drinks at home. Finally, Starbucks competes with traditional coffee producers including Folgers, Maxwell House, and Eight O'Clock Coffee.

Because competition is customer specific, companies that compete in one market can collaborate in another. For example, Apple competes with Microsoft in the market for personal computers and tablets while also collaborating with it to develop productivity software, including word processing and spreadsheet programs.

Collaborators

Collaborators are entities that work with the company to create value for target customers. The choice of collaborators is driven by the complementarity of the resources needed to fulfill customer needs. Collaboration involves outsourcing (rather than developing) the resources that the company lacks and that are required to fulfill the needs of target customers. Thus, instead of building or acquiring resources that are lacking, a company can "borrow" them by partnering with entities that have these resources and can benefit from sharing them.

For example, Starbucks collaborates with numerous coffee growers around the globe to provide high-quality coffee beans. Starbucks also partners with suppliers that provide various non-coffee items such as water, pastries, snacks, and branded merchandise. In addition, Starbucks collaborates with a variety of retail outlets including grocery chains, mass-merchandisers, warehouse clubs, and convenience stores that sell Starbucks coffee beans, instant coffee, and snacks.

Common types of collaborators include suppliers, manufacturers, distributors (dealers, wholesalers, and retailers), research-and-development entities, service providers, external sales force, advertising agencies, and marketing research companies. For example, Procter & Gamble collaborates with the design firm IDEO to develop some of its products, with Diamond Packaging to provide packaging, and with retail giant Walmart for distribution. Walmart collaborates with Procter & Gamble to procure many of its products, with software solutions provider Oracle to streamline its logistics, and with shipping conglomerate Moller-Maersk to transport its goods.

Company

The company is the entity that develops and manages a given market offering. The company can be a manufacturer that produces the actual goods being sold (Procter & Gamble), a service provider (American Express), an entity engaged in brand building (Lacoste), a media company (Facebook), or a retailer (Walmart). The company is not limited to a single role; it can perform multiple functions. For example, a retailer might have its own production facility, engage in building its own brand, and offer a variety of value-added services.

In the case of enterprises with diverse strategic competencies and market offerings, the term *company* refers to the particular business unit (also called the *strategic business unit*) of the organization managing the specific offering. For example, GE, Alphabet (Google's parent company), and Facebook have multiple strategic business units, each of which can be viewed as a separate company requiring its own business model.

A company's motivation and ability to create market value can be defined by two main factors: *profile* and *goals*.

- **Profile** reflects the company's characteristics, including the resources that determine its ability to create market value and a sustainable competitive advantage. A company's resources include factors such as business facilities; suppliers; employees; know-how; existing products, services, and brands; communication and distribution channels; and access to capital.

- **Goals** reflect the end result that the company aims to achieve with a particular offering. Company goals can be monetary, such as maximizing profits, and strategic, such as establishing synergies with other company offerings and creating value for society at large.

For example, Starbucks' profile is defined by its numerous retail locations, its relationships with coffee growers and distributors, its professionally trained employees, its intellectual property, its strong brand, its loyal customer base, and its access to capital markets. Starbucks' monetary goal — to generate revenues and profits for its shareholders — is complemented by its strategic goal to benefit society and promote social responsibility.

Context

Context describes the environment in which the company operates. It is defined by five factors:

- **Sociocultural context** includes social and demographic trends, value systems, religion, language, lifestyles, attitudes, and beliefs.

- **Technological context** includes new techniques, skills, methods, and processes for designing, manufacturing, communicating, and delivering market offerings.

- **Regulatory context** includes taxes; import tariffs; embargoes; product specification, pricing, and communication regulations; and intellectual property laws.

- **Economic context** includes economic growth, money supply, inflation, and interest rates.

- Physical context includes natural resources, climate, geographic location, topography, and health trends.

For example, Starbucks' context is characterized by the growing popularity of crafted coffee drinks and the desire to socialize in person, as well as by the growing popularity of online communications; by the technological developments that enable the company to better understand its customers, track their buying behavior, and communicate with them on a one-on-one basis; by the favorable trade agreements that influence import tariffs on coffee; by various economic factors, including the state of the local economy and the global commodity prices for coffee; and by the climate and weather patterns across different geographic locations.

Marketing Strategy: Developing a Value Proposition

The value proposition defines the value that an offering aims to create for the relevant market entities. The key to designing a meaningful value proposition is to understand the value exchange defining the relationships among the different market participants. The key aspects of developing a value proposition are discussed below.

Defining the Value Exchange

The value proposition defines the value that an offering aims to create for market participants. Designing a meaningful value proposition calls for understanding the *value exchange* among the relevant market entities — customers, the company, its collaborators, and its competitors — that operate in a given context (Figure 2). Accordingly, the value exchange defines how different entities create and capture value in a given market.

Figure 2. Defining the Value Exchange

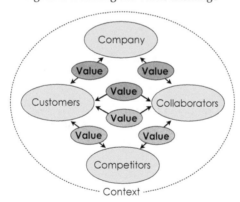

Each of the relationships defining the value exchange is a process of giving (creating) and receiving (capturing) value. Thus, the relationship between the company and its customers is defined by the value the company creates for its customers as well as by the value created by these customers that is captured by the company. The relationship between the company and its collaborators is defined by the value the company creates for these collaborators as well as by the value generated by these collaborators that is captured by the company. The relationship between the company's customers and its collaborators is defined by the value these collaborators create for target customers as well as by the value generated by the target customers that is captured by collaborators.

To illustrate, consider the relationship between a manufacturer, a retailer, and their customers. The manufacturer (the company) partners with a retailer (the collaborator) to deliver an offering to target customers. *Customers* receive value from the product (created by the manufacturer) they purchase as well as from the service (delivered by the retailer) involved in the buying process, for which they offer monetary compensation that is shared by both the manufacturer and the retailer. The *retailer* receives value from customers in the form of margins (the differential between the buying and selling price) as well as value from the manufacturer in the form of various trade promotions. The *manufacturer* receives value from customers in the form of the price they pay for its products (excluding the retailer markup) as well as from the retailer in the form of the various services performed by the retailer on the manufacturer's behalf.

The three value relationships between the company, its customers, and its collaborators reflect only the company side of the value exchange. No market exists without competitors that aim to create value for the same target customers, often working with the same collaborators as the company. The competitive aspect of the value exchange mirrors the company side of the value exchange. Specifically, it consists of three types of value relationships: those between the company's target customers and its competitors, those between the company's target customers and competitors' collaborators (some or all of whom could also be the company's collaborators), and those between the competitors and their collaborators. To succeed in a competitive environment, a company must deliver superior value to its target customers and collaborators in a way that enables the company to achieve its own goals.

The Market Value Principle

To succeed, an offering must create superior value for all relevant entities involved in the market exchange—target customers, collaborators, and the company. Accordingly, when developing market offerings, a company needs to consider all three types of value: *customer value, collaborator value,* and *company value.*

- Customer value is the worth of an offering to its customers; it is customers' assessment of the degree to which an offering fulfills their needs. The value an offering creates for its customers is determined by three main factors: (1) the *needs* of these customers, (2) the benefits and costs of the company's offering, and (3) the benefits and costs of the alternative means (competitive offerings) target customers can use to fulfill their needs. Simply put, the customer value proposition answers the question: *Why would target customers choose the company's offering instead of the available alternatives?*

- Collaborator value is the worth of an offering to the company's collaborators; it is the sum of all benefits and costs that an offering creates for collaborators. The collaborator value proposition reflects an offering's ability to help collaborators achieve their goals better than the alternative offerings. Simply put, the collaborator value proposition answers the question: *Why would collaborators choose the company's offering instead of the competitive alternatives?*

- Company value is the worth of the offering to the company; it is the sum of all benefits and costs associated with an offering. The value of an offering is defined relative to the company's goal and the value of other opportunities that are available to the company, such as the value of other offerings that could be launched by the company. The company value proposition answers the question: *Why would the company choose this offering instead of the alternative options?*

Creating value for target customers, collaborators, and the company is the overarching principle that guides all company actions; it is the *market value principle* that encapsulates the company's value proposition:

> The offering must create superior value for its target customers and collaborators in a way that enables the company to achieve its goals

Because the market value principle underscores the importance of creating value for the three key entities — target customers, the company, and collaborators, it is also referred to as the 3-V principle. The market value principle means that the viability of a business model is defined by the answers to three sets of questions:

What value does the offering create for its target customers? Why would target customers choose this offering? What makes this offering better than the alternative options?

What value does the offering create for the company's collaborators? Why would the entities identified as collaborators (suppliers, distributors, and co-developers) partner with the company?

What value does the offering create for the company? Why should the company invest resources in this offering rather than in an alternative offering?

The need to manage value for three different entities raises the question of whose value to prioritize. Surprisingly, many companies find it difficult to reach a consensus. Marketing departments are typically focused on creating customer value; finance departments and senior management are focused on creating company (shareholder) value; and the sales force is focused on creating value for collaborators, such as dealers, wholesalers, and retailers.

The "right" answer is that the company needs to balance the value among its stakeholders, customers, and collaborators to create an optimal value proposition. Here, the term *optimal value* means that the value of the offering is balanced across the three entities, such that it creates value for target customers and collaborators in a way that enables the company to achieve its strategic goals. Optimizing customer, company, and collaborator value is the market value principle, which is the cornerstone of market success (Figure 3). Failure to create superior value for any of these entities inevitably leads to an unsustainable business model and failure of the business venture.

Figure 3. The 3-V Market Value Principle

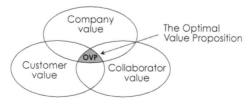

To illustrate, consider the ways in which Starbucks creates market value. Customers receive the functional benefit of a variety of coffee beverages as well as the psychological benefit of expressing certain aspects of their personality through the choice of a customized beverage, for which they deliver monetary compensation. Starbucks collaborators (coffee growers) receive monetary payments for the coffee beans they provide and the strategic benefit of having a consistent demand for their product, in return for which they invest resources in growing coffee beans that conform to Starbucks' standards. By investing resources in developing and offering its products and services to consumers, the company (Starbucks) derives monetary benefit (revenues and profits) and the strategic benefits of building a brand and enhancing its market footprint.

The value proposition reflects the company's expectation of the value that the offering will create for the three key market entities. The value proposition does not physically exist in the market. Rather, value is created by specific offering(s) the company and its collaborators design, communicate, and deliver to target customers. The key aspects of developing offering(s) that create market value are discussed in the following section.

Marketing Tactics: Designing the Market Offering

The market offering is the actual good that the company deploys in order to fulfill a particular customer need. Unlike the target market and the value proposition, which reflect the company's strategy, the market offering reflects the company's tactics — the specific way in which the company will create value in the market in which it competes.

The Seven Attributes Defining the Market Offering

A company's offering is defined by seven attributes: product, service, brand, price, incentives, communication, and distribution. These seven attributes are also referred to as the *marketing mix* — the combination of specific activities employed to execute the offering's strategy. These seven tactics defining the offering are the tools that managers have at their disposal to create market value (Figure 4).

Figure 4. Marketing Tactics: The Seven Attributes Defining the Market Offering

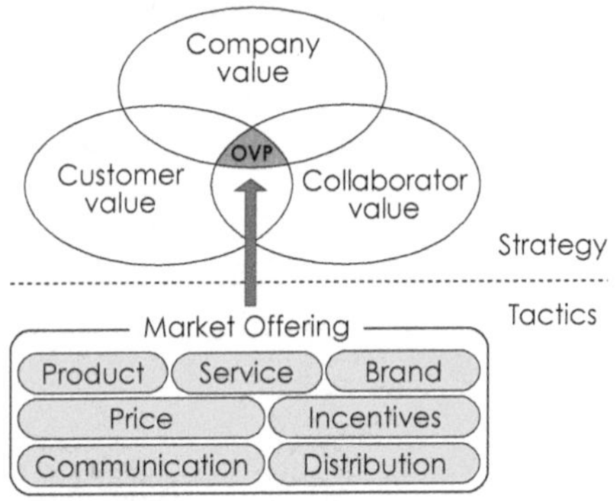

The seven attributes that delineate the market offering are defined as follows:

- The **product** is a good that aims to create value for target customers. Products can be both tangible (e.g., food, apparel, and automobiles) and intangible (e.g., software, music, and video). Products entitle customers to the rights to the acquired good. For example, a customer purchasing a car or a software program takes ownership of the acquired product.

- The **service** is a good that aims to create value for its customers without entitling them to ownership of this good (e.g., movie rental, appliance repairs, medical procedures, and tax preparation). The same offering might be positioned as a product or a service. For example, a software program can be offered as a product, with customers purchasing the rights to a copy of the program, or as a service, with customers renting the program to temporarily receive its benefits.

- The **brand** aims to identify the company's products and services, differentiate them from those of the competition, and create unique value beyond the product and service aspects of the offering. For example, the Harley-Davidson brand identifies its motorcycles; differentiates these motorcycles from those made by Honda, Suzuki, Kawasaki, and Yamaha; and elicits a distinct emotional reaction from its customers, who use Harley-Davidson's brand to express their individuality.

- The **price** is the amount of money the company charges its customers and collaborators for the benefits provided by the offering.

- **Incentives** are tools that enhance the value of the offering by reducing its costs and/or by increasing its benefits. Common incentives include volume discounts, price reductions, coupons, rebates, premiums, bonus offerings, contests, and rewards. Incentives can be offered to individual customers as well as to the company's collaborators (e.g., incentives given to channel partners).

- **Communication** informs the relevant market entities — target customers, collaborators, and the company — about the specifics of the offering.

- **Distribution** involves the channel(s) used to deliver the offering to target customers and the company's collaborators.

To illustrate, consider the attributes of Starbucks' offering. The *product* is the variety of coffee and other beverages, as well as food items available. The *service* is the assistance offered to customers prior to, during, and after purchase. The *brand* is Starbucks' name, logo, and the associations it evokes in customers' minds. The *price* is the monetary amount that Starbucks charges customers for its offerings. *Incentives* are the promotional tools — loyalty program, coupons, and temporary price reductions — that provide additional benefits for customers. *Communication* is the information disseminated via different media channels — advertising, social media, and public relations — informing the public about Starbucks' offerings. *Distribution* includes both the Starbucks-owned stores and Starbucks-licensed retail outlets, through which Starbucks' offerings are delivered to its customers.

Marketing Tactics as a Process of Designing, Communicating, and Delivering Value

The seven marketing tactics—product, service, brand, price, incentives, communication, and distribution—can be viewed as a *process of designing, communicating, and delivering* customer value. The product, service, brand, price, and incentives are the value-design aspect of the offering; communication is the process of communicating value; and distribution is the value-delivery aspect of the offering (Figure 5). Customer value is created across all three dimensions, with different attributes playing distinct roles in the value-creation process.

Figure 5. Marketing Tactics as a Process of Designing, Communicating, and Delivering Customer Value

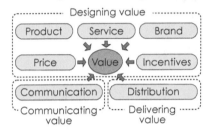

Because they define the key benefits and costs, the product, service, brand, price, and incentives are the *key value drivers* of the offering. Communication and distribution are the channels through which the benefits created by the first five attributes are communicated and delivered to target customers. Thus, communication informs customers about the functionality of a product or service, builds the image of its brand, publicizes its price, apprises buyers of sales promotions, and advises them about the availability of the offering. Likewise, distribution delivers a company's products and services, delivers customer payments to the company, and delivers the offering's promotional incentives to customers and collaborators.

The value-creation process can be examined from both the company and customer perspectives. From a company's perspective, value creation is a process of *designing, communicating*, and *delivering* value. From a customer's perspective, however, the value-creation process can be viewed in terms of the *attractiveness, awareness*, and *availability* of the offering.[2] Thus, an offering's ability to create customer value is determined by the answers to the following three questions:

What makes the offering attractive to target customers?

How will target customers become aware of the offering?

How will target customers acquire the offering?

The answer to the first question outlines the customer benefits and costs associated with the product, service, brand, price, and incentives aspects of the offering. The answer to the second question outlines the way in which the company will communicate the specifics of the offering to its target customers. The answer to the third question outlines the way in which the company will make the offering available to its target customers. In this context, the customer-centric approach to managing the *attractiveness, awareness*, and *availability* of an offering complements the company-centric approach of managing the process of *designing, communicating*, and *delivering* value to target customers (Figure 6).

Figure 6. Marketing Tactics: Company Actions and Customer Impact

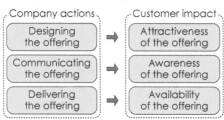

To illustrate, consider the process of designing, communicating, and delivering value in the case of Starbucks. The product aspect of Starbucks' offerings involves designing its portfolio of products—espressos, lattes, macchiatos, and frappuccinos—informing and educating customers about these drinks, and then physically delivering them to customers. The service aspect of the offering involves defining the level of service that Starbucks wants to offer customers, communicating its service policies (such as the promise that a customer's drink will be perfect every time), and ultimately delivering the service to its customers. Building the Starbucks brand involves selecting the brand name, designing the logo, defining what the Starbucks brand should mean to its customers (Starbucks' goal is to become the "third place" in people's daily lives, after home and work), and then communicating and delivering this meaning to target customers. Managing the price involves setting prices for all possible combinations of its various drinks and sizes, communicating these prices to consumers, and collecting consumer payments. Finally, managing incentives involves deciding what, when, and how many sales promotions to offer (such as discounts on certain drinks, 2-for-1 promotions, and loyalty programs), communicating these incentives, and delivering them to target customers using appropriate channels (e.g., newspaper inserts, online banner advertisements, and proximity-based mobile promotions).

The Market Value Map

For practical purposes, the strategy and tactics delineating a company's business model can be represented as a value map that outlines the ways in which an offering creates value for its target customers, collaborators, and the company. The market value map is a schematic presentation of the business model, enabling managers to clearly articulate the key aspects of the company's strategy and tactics. Thus, the primary purpose of the value map is to visually outline the key aspects of the business model and serve as a guide that lays out the company's strategy and tactics.

The market value map follows the structure of the business model and comprises three key components—*the target market, the value proposition,* and *the market offering*—that define the offering's strategy and tactics. Accordingly, the market value map is visually represented as a matrix: The left side outlines the key elements of the company's strategy—the target market (customers, collaborators, company, competitors, and context) and the value proposition (customer value, collaborator value, and company value)—and the right side outlines the market offering defined by its seven key attributes (product, service, brand, price, incentives, communication, and distribution). The components of the market value map and the key questions defining each component are shown in Figure 7.

Figure 7. The Market Value Map

Target Market	
Customers	What customer need does the company aim to fulfill? Who are the customers with this need?
Collaborators	What other entities will work with the company to fulfill the identified customer need?
Company	What are the company's resources that will enable it to fulfill the identified customer need?
Competition	What other offerings aim to fulfill the same need of the same target customers?
Context	What are the sociocultural, technological, regulatory, economic, and physical aspects of the environment?

Market Offering	
Product	What are the key features of the company's product?
Service	What are the key features of the company's service?
Brand	What are the key features of the offering's brand?
Price	What is the offering's price?
Incentives	What incentives does the offering provide?
Communication	How will target customers and collaborators become aware of the company's offering?
Distribution	How will the offering be delivered to target customers and collaborators?

Value Proposition	
Customer Value	What value does the offering create for target customers?
Collaborator Value	What value does the offering create for the company's collaborators?
Company Value	What value does the offering create for the company?

⬆ Strategy   ⬆ Tactics

The market value map outlines the ways in which an offering creates value for the three relevant market entities—customers, collaborators, and the company. Because each of these entities requires its own value proposition and employs different tools to create value, the market value map can be represented as three separate maps: the customer value map, the collaborator value map, and the company value map.

These three value maps depict a company's business model from the viewpoint of each of the three market entities involved in the value-creation process. The *customer value map* reflects the way an offering creates value for target customers, the *collaborator value map* reflects the way an offering creates value for the company's collaborators, and the *company value map* reflects the way an offering creates value for the company.

The G-STIC Framework for Marketing Management

The marketing strategy and tactics do not exist in a vacuum: They are integral components of a company's marketing plan, which delineates the company's ultimate goal and the ways in which it aims to achieve this goal. The marketing plan presents a company's business activities in a logical and structured way to provide guidelines for managers and enable the company to implement its business model.

The backbone of the marketing plan is the action plan, which defines the company's goal and a course of action to reach this goal. The development of an action plan is guided by five key activities: setting a *goal*, developing a *strategy*, designing the *tactics*, defining an *implementation* plan, and identifying a set of *control* metrics to measure the success of the proposed action. These five activities comprise the G-STIC (Goal-Strategy-Tactics-Implementation-Control) framework, which is the cornerstone of marketing planning and analysis (Figure 8). The core of the action plan is the business model comprising the offering's strategy and tactics.

Figure 8. The G-STIC Framework for Marketing Management

The individual components of the G-STIC framework are outlined in more detail below.

- The **goal** identifies the ultimate criterion for success; it is the end result that the company aims to achieve. The goal has two components: the *focus*, which defines the metric reflecting the desired outcome of the company's actions (e.g., net income), and the performance *benchmarks* quantifying the goal and defining the time frame for it to be accomplished.

- The **strategy** defines the company's *target market* and its *value proposition* in this market. The strategy is the backbone of the company's business model.

- **Tactics** define the key attributes of the company's offering: *product, service, brand, price, incentives, communication,* and *distribution*. These seven tactics are the tools that the company uses to create value in the chosen market.

- **Implementation** defines the processes involved in creating the market offering. Implementation includes *developing* the offering and *deploying* the offering in the target market.

- **Control** evaluates the success of the company's activities over time by evaluating the company's *performance* and monitoring the changes in the market *environment* in which the company operates.

The key components of the marketing plan and the key factors describing each component are outlined in Figure 9.

Figure 9. The G-STIC Action-Planning Flowchart

Goal	The ultimate criterion for success
Focus — Benchmarks	
Strategy	The value created in the target market
Target market — Value proposition	
Tactics	The specifics of the market offering
Product — Service — Brand	
Price — Incentives	
Communication — Distribution	
Implementation	The logistics of creating the offering
Development — Deployment	
Control	Monitoring goal progress
Performance — Environment	

The G-STIC framework offers an intuitive approach to streamlining a company's activities into a logical sequence that aims to produce the desired market outcome. Note that even though the G-STIC framework implies a particular sequence, starting with the definition of the company's goal and concluding with identifying controls for measuring performance, marketing planning is an iterative process. Thus, the development of a marketing plan often starts with the identification of an unmet customer need that the company can fulfill better than the competition. The development of a marketing plan can also start with a technological invention that enables the company to create market value. In this context, the G-STIC framework describes the key elements of the iterative process of marketing planning (Goal, Strategy, Tactics, Implementation, and Control) and outlines a logical sequence of organizing these elements without prescribing the order in which these elements are developed.

The marketing planning process is formalized as a written document that effectively communicates the proposed course of action to relevant stakeholders: company employees, collaborators, shareholders, and investors. Writing a marketing plan is different from marketing planning. Marketing planning is the *process* of identifying a goal and developing a course of action to achieve this goal. The marketing plan is the tangible *outcome* of a company's marketing planning process that documents an already identified goal and the decided-on course of action. The key aspects of writing a marketing plan are outlined in the following chapter.

Additional Readings

Chernev, Alexander (2018), *Strategic Marketing Management* (9th ed.). Chicago, IL: Cerebellum Press.

Kotler, Philip and Kevin Lane Keller (2016), *Marketing Management* (15th ed.). Upper Saddle River, NJ: Prentice Hall.

Lehmann, Donald R. and Russell S. Winer (2007), *Analysis for Marketing Planning* (7th ed.). Boston, MA: McGraw-Hill/Irwin.

CHAPTER THREE

WRITING A MARKETING PLAN

A goal without a plan is just a wish.
— Antoine de Saint-Exupéry,
French writer, author of *The Little Prince*

The marketing plan presents a company's business activities in a logical and structured way to provide guidelines for managers and enable the company to implement the proposed course of action. The key aspects of developing an actionable marketing plan are discussed in more detail in this chapter and are illustrated with stylized examples presented in Chapters 4–6.

Overview

A company's marketing plan serves a dual purpose. First, the marketing plan aims to *guide* a company's actions to enable the company to reach its goals. The second purpose of the marketing plan is to *inform* the relevant entities about the company's goal and the proposed course of action in order to ensure that all stakeholders are on the same page with respect to the company's activities.

Most marketing plans follow a similar structure: They start with an executive summary, followed by a situation overview and an action plan, and conclude with a set of exhibits offering additional information related to the proposed course of action.

The core of the marketing plan is the action plan, which is organized around the G-STIC framework. The starting point of the action plan is an outline of the company goals. The goal outline is followed by a description of the company's strategy, which defines the target market(s) and the offering's value proposition for target customers, the company, and its collaborators. The strategy is followed by a description of the marketing tactics — product, service, brand, price, incentives, communication, and distribution. The tactics are then followed by an implementation plan that describes the process of turning the proposed strategy and tactics into reality. Finally, the control aspect of action planning outlines a policy for evaluating the company's performance and analyzing the environment to ensure adequate progress toward the set goal.

The key components of the marketing plan are illustrated in Figure 1 and discussed in more detail in the following sections. The key aspects of the marketing plan are further illustrated with stylized examples presented in Chapters 4–6.

Figure 1. The Marketing Plan

Executive Summary		
What are the key aspects of the company's marketing plan?		

Situation Overview		
Company What are the company's history, culture, resources, offerings, and ongoing activities?		**Market** What are the key aspects of the markets in which the company competes?

Goal		
Focus What is the key performance metric the company aims to achieve with the offering?		**Benchmarks** What are the criteria (temporal and quantitative) for reaching the goal?

Strategy		
Target market Who are the target customers, competitors, and collaborators? What are the company's resources and context?		**Value proposition** What is the company's value proposition for target customers, collaborators, and the company?

Tactics		
Market offering What are the product, service, brand, price, incentives, communication, and distribution aspects of the offering?		

Implementation		
Development How is the company offering being developed?		**Deployment** What processes will be used to bring the offering to market?

Control		
Performance How will the company evaluate the progress toward its goal?		**Environment** How will the company monitor the environment to identify new opportunities and threats?

Exhibits		
What are the details/evidence supporting the company's action plan?		

- The **executive summary** is the "elevator pitch" for the marketing plan—a streamlined and succinct overview of the company's goal and the proposed course of action. The typical executive summary is one or two pages long and does not discuss the specifics of the action plan.

- The **situation overview** section of the marketing plan provides an overall evaluation of the company and the markets in which it competes and/or will compete. Accordingly, the situation overview involves two sections: the *company overview*, which outlines the company's history, culture, resources (competencies and assets), and its portfolio of offerings, and the *market overview*, which outlines the markets in which the company operates and/or could potentially target.

- The **goal** section of the marketing plan identifies the desired outcome that the company aims to achieve, as well as the specific quantitative and temporal benchmarks characterizing this outcome.

- The **strategy** section of the marketing plan outlines the blueprint for achieving the company's goal. This section involves two key components: It describes the target market for the company's offering and defines the offering's value proposition.

- The **tactics** section of the marketing plan delineates how the desired strategy will be translated into a set of specific actions. This section defines seven key decisions that managers need to make with respect to the market offering: product, service, brand, price, incentives, communication, and distribution.

- The **implementation** section of the marketing plan outlines the processes by which the company's strategy and tactics are transformed into an offering that is ultimately introduced in the market. Specifically, this section outlines the main aspects of implementing a company's strategy and tactics: developing the infrastructure, developing the offering, and commercial deployment.

- The **control** section of the action plan outlines the procedures that evaluate the company's performance and analyze the environment in which it operates.

- **Exhibits** help streamline the logic of the marketing plan by separating the less important and/or more technical aspects of the plan into a distinct section in the form of tables, charts, and appendices.

Because the key purpose of the marketing plan is to guide a company's actions, the core of the marketing plan is defined by the G-STIC framework that delineates the company's goal and the proposed course of action. The other elements of the marketing plan—the executive summary, situation overview, and exhibits—aim to facilitate an understanding of the logic underlying the plan and provide specifics of the proposed course of action. The key components of the marketing plan are discussed in more detail in the following sections.

Executive Summary

The executive summary is a concise overview of the proposed course of action. The executive summary presents the gist of the marketing plan in a way that makes the goal, as well as the key aspects of the proposed action, transparent to the reader. The typical executive summary consists of five main components: *introduction, situation overview, goal, action overview, and conclusion*. These five aspects of the executive summary are briefly outlined below.

- The **introduction** typically identifies the primary purpose of the proposed course of action—the opportunity the company aims to take advantage of or the problem/threat it aims to address—and the key aspects of the company's action plan. The introduction aims to situate the company's offering in a reader's mind in order to frame the subsequently presented information and facilitate the understanding of the specifics of the plan.

- The **situation overview** section of the executive summary identifies a promising opportunity, an impending threat, and/or a gap in a company's performance. The situation overview component of the executive summary should be concise, focusing on those aspects of the situation that are pertinent to the proposed course of action.

- The **goal** component of the executive summary outlines the desired outcome of the company's action and its quantitative and temporal benchmarks. When necessary, the description of the primary goal can be complemented by a discussion of some of the key specific objectives that pave the way for achieving this goal (for example, what changes need to occur in the behavior of the target customers in order for the company to achieve its profit goal).

- The **action overview** section of the executive summary outlines the most important aspects of the proposed course of action. It typically identifies the key aspects of the target market in which the company will compete, the value proposition for the relevant market entities, and the key aspects of the market offering.

- The **conclusion** section of the executive summary presents the key takeaways of the marketing plan. The conclusion typically does not introduce new information. Instead, it highlights the important aspects of the already presented information to reaffirm the proposed course of action.

The key to writing a meaningful executive summary is to present the information in a way that allows a reader unfamiliar with the offering to grasp the essence of the proposed course of action. Depending on the complexity of the marketing plan, the executive summary can take anywhere from half a page to two or three pages. A detailed example of a marketing plan's executive summary is given in Section 1 in Chapters 4–6.

Situation Overview

The situation overview delineates the key aspects of the market in which the company currently competes and/or in which it might compete in the future. The situation overview aims to set the stage for the marketing plan by providing the relevant background necessary for understanding the rationale for the proposed course of action. Providing such background information is important because some of the readers of the marketing plan might not be familiar with the specifics of the market or might not readily relate their prior knowledge to the problem at hand.

The situation overview section is typically organized into two parts: *company overview* and *market overview*. These two aspects of the situation overview are outlined in more detail below and a detailed example of the situation overview section of a marketing plan is given in Section 2 in Chapters 4–6.

Company Overview

The company overview provides information about the company, including its vision, strategic goals, current performance, core competencies, strategic assets, opportunities, and threats. This overview can be done on the level of a strategic business unit (e.g., a division of the company) or on a more general level that includes the entire company.

- **Goals and current performance.** This section outlines the company's long-term vision and strategic goals. It also outlines the company's progress toward its goals and, when relevant, identifies the key performance gaps.

- **Strategic analysis.** An important component of the company overview is evaluating its competitive advantages and disadvantages. A common approach to conducting this analysis involves evaluating a company's resources — core competencies and strategic assets — in order to identify the company's strengths and weaknesses.

Market Overview

The market overview provides an overview of the market in which the company operates. A common approach to conducting market analysis involves evaluating four factors: *customers*, *collaborators*, *competitors*, and *context*:

- **Customers** are the current and potential buyers of the offerings furnished by the company and its competitors. The term "customers" used in this section has broader meaning than its use in the subsequent sections of the marketing plan, where it refers only to the customers that are actually targeted by the company.

- **Collaborators** are entities that work or could potentially work with the company to create the offering, communicate its benefits, and/or deliver the offering to customers. The term "collaborators" used in this section has broader meaning than its use in the subsequent sections of the marketing plan, where it refers only to the entities that actually work with the company.

- **Competitors** are entities with offerings that cater to the same customers and aim to fulfill the same customer need as the company does.

- **Context** defines the environment in which the company and its competitors operate. This environment is defined by five factors: *economic* (economic growth, money supply, inflation, and interest rates); *technological* (the diffusion of existing technologies and the development of new ones); *sociocultural* (demographic trends, value systems, and market-specific beliefs and behavior); *regulatory* (import/export tariffs, taxes, product specifications, pricing and advertising policies, and patent and trademark protection); and *physical* (natural resources, climate, and health conditions).

Note that the market overview section might not necessarily address all five "C"s — company, customers, collaborators, competitors, and context. Because it aims to provide the background for understanding the logic of the proposed course of action, the market overview highlights only the relevant aspects of the market.

The situation overview often relies on the SWOT framework, which calls for evaluating four key factors — strengths, weaknesses, opportunities, and threats — that define a company's competitive position in the market. Here strengths and weaknesses reflect favorable and unfavorable factors that are *internal* to the company (e.g., core competencies and strategic assets), and are a part of the company overview. In contrast, opportunities and threats reflect favorable and unfavorable factors that are *external* to the company and are determined by the market (customers, collaborators, competitors, and context) in which the company operates. Accordingly, the analysis of opportunities and threats is a part of the market overview section of the situation overview. The SWOT framework is discussed in more detail in Appendix F.

Goal

The goal section of the marketing plan outlines the desired outcome that the company aims to achieve. The goal guides all the company's marketing activities; without a well-defined goal, an organization cannot design an effective marketing strategy and evaluate the success of its current activities.

Setting a goal involves two decisions: identifying the *focus* of the company's actions and defining the specific quantitative and temporal *benchmarks* to be reached. In addition, the goal section of the marketing plan can identify the specific *market objectives* that need to be achieved in order to achieve the company's primary goal. These aspects of the goal are outlined below, and a detailed example is given in Section 3 in Chapters 4–6.

Goal Focus

The focus of the goal identifies the key criterion for a company's success; it is the metric describing the desired outcome. Based on their focus, there are two types of goals: *monetary* and *strategic*.

- **Monetary goals** involve monetary outcomes and typically focus on maximizing net income, earnings per share, and return on investment. Monetary goals are common for offerings managed by for-profit companies.

- **Strategic goals** involve nonmonetary outcomes that are of strategic importance to the company. Strategic goals are common for both nonprofit organizations (e.g., promoting social welfare) and for-profit organizations (e.g., facilitating the achievement of monetary goals). Thus, a strategic goal might involve promoting an offering that, although not profitable by itself, benefits the company by facilitating the sales of other, profit-generating offerings. A strategic goal might also involve enhancing the corporate culture (e.g., by boosting employee morale and by facilitating employee recruitment and retention), thus indirectly contributing to the company's bottom line.

Monetary goals and strategic goals are not mutually exclusive: A company might aim to achieve strategic goals with a profitable offering, and a strategically important offering might ultimately contribute to the company's bottom line. In fact, long-term financial planning typically includes a strategic component in addition to the monetary goal, and long-term strategic planning typically includes a financial component that articulates how achieving a particular strategic goal will translate into a positive financial outcome.

Performance Benchmarks

Performance benchmarks define the ultimate criteria for success. The two types of performance benchmarks—*quantitative* and *temporal*—are discussed in more detail below.

- **Quantitative benchmarks** define the specific milestones to be achieved by the company with respect to its focal goal. For example, goals such as "increase market share by 2%," "increase retention rates by 12%," and "improve the effectiveness of marketing expenditures by 15%" include benchmarks that quantify the goal. Quantitative benchmarks can be expressed in either relative terms (e.g., increase market share by 20%) or absolute terms (e.g., achieve annual sales of one million units).

- **Temporal benchmarks** identify the time frame for achieving a particular mile-stone. Setting a timeline for achieving a goal is an important strategic decision, because the course of action adopted to implement this goal is often contingent on the time horizon. For example, the goal of maximizing next-quarter profits will likely require a different strategy and tactics than the goal of maximizing long-term profitability.

To illustrate, a company's goal might involve generating net income (focus) of $1 billion (quantitative benchmark) by the end of the fiscal year (temporal benchmark).

Market Objectives

Based on their focus, goals vary in their level of generality. Some goals reflect outcomes that are more fundamental than others. Therefore, a company's goals can be represented as a hierarchy headed by a company's primary goal, which is implemented through a set of more specific goals, referred to as market objectives.

Unlike the primary goal, which is typically defined in terms of a company-focused outcome, market objectives delineate specific changes in the behavior of the relevant market factors—customers, the company, collaborators, competitors, and context—that will enable the company to achieve its primary goal. The different types of market objectives are outlined below.

- **Customer objectives** aim to elicit changes in the behavior of target customers (e.g., increasing purchase frequency, switching from a competitive product, or making a first-time purchase in a product category) that will enable the company to achieve its primary goal. To illustrate, the company goal of increasing net revenues can be associated with the more specific objective of increasing the frequency with which its customers repurchase the offering. Because the customers are the ultimate source of a company's revenues and profits, a company's primary goal typically involves a customer-focused objective.

- **Collaborator objectives** aim to elicit changes in the behavior of the company's collaborators, such as providing greater promotional support, better pricing terms, greater systems integration, and extended distribution coverage. To illustrate, the company goal of increasing net revenues can be associated with the more specific collaborator objective of increasing the shelf space for the offering in distribution channels.

- **Company (internal) objectives** aim to elicit changes in the company's own actions, such as improving product and service quality, reducing the cost of goods sold, improving the effectiveness of the company's marketing actions, and streamlining research-and-development costs.

- **Competitive objectives** aim to change the behavior of the company's competitors. Such actions might involve creating barriers to entry, securing proprietary access to scarce resources, and circumventing a price war.

- **Context objectives** are less common and usually implemented by larger companies that have the resources to influence the economic, technological, sociocultural, regulatory, and/or physical context in which the company operates. For example, a company might lobby the government to adopt regulations that will favorably affect the company by offering tax benefits, offering subsidies, and imposing import duties on competitors' products.

Defining market objectives is important because without a change in the behavior of the relevant market entities or the context in which the company operates, the company is unlikely to enhance its ability to reach the ultimate goal. Thus, by identifying specific domains in which action is needed, market objectives help the company zero in on the specific course of action aimed at achieving its primary goal.

To illustrate, a company's primary goal of increasing net income by $1B by the end of the fiscal year can involve different objectives. A customer-specific objective might involve increasing market share by 10% by the end of the fiscal year. A collaborator-related objective might involve securing 45% of the distribution outlets by the end of the third quarter. An internal objective might involve lowering the cost of goods sold by 25% by the end of the first quarter.

Strategy

The strategy section of the marketing plan outlines the master plan for achieving the company's goal. Delineating an offering's strategy involves two key components: defining the offering's *target market* and defining the offering's *value proposition*. These two components of strategy development are discussed in more detail below and a detailed example is given in Section 4 in Chapters 4–6.

Target Market

The target market is defined by its five key components: (1) target customers, (2) the company (or the business unit responsible for the offering), (3) collaborators, (4) competitors, and (5) context (Five Cs). Although both the market overview and the target market sections of the marketing plan involve analysis of these factors, the target market analysis is much narrower and includes only markets that are targeted by the company. The key aspects of this market—*target customers, company, collaborators, competitors, and context*—are discussed in more detail below.

- **Target Customers.** The target customer section of the marketing plan defines the buyers for whom the company will tailor its offering. Identifying target customers involves identifying *customer value*, which focuses on the customer needs that the company aims to fulfill with its offering, and identifying the *customer profile*, which depicts the observable demographic and behavioral characteristics of the value-based customer segments that will enable the company to reach these customers in an effective and cost-efficient manner. Because creating value is central to the success of an offering, value-based targeting is the backbone of identifying target customers, whereas profile-based targeting facilitates the identification of customers for the purposes of communicating and delivering the offering to these customers.

- **Company.** The company section of the marketing plan defines the entity that manages the offering. This entity can be the entire company (in the case of single-offering companies) or a strategic business unit (e.g., department, division, or branch) within the company. The company overview often involves an outline of the company's core competencies and strategic assets.

- **Collaborators.** The collaborator section identifies entities that work with the company to design, communicate, and deliver value to target customers. Collaboration can involve areas such as product design, service development, branding, pricing, incentives management, communication, and distribution. For example, a company can collaborate to develop a product (research-and-development collaboration), create a customer incentive (promotional collaboration), and deliver the offering to the customer (channel collaboration).

- **Competitors.** The competitor section identifies current and potential competitors that target the same customers and aim to fulfill the same customer need as the company's offering. Because competitors are defined relative to the needs of target customers, the competition often goes beyond the traditional industry-defined categories to include cross-category offerings that could fulfill the same customer need.

- **Context.** The context section outlines the relevant aspects of the *economic* (economic growth, money supply, inflation, and interest rates); *technological* (the diffusion of existing technologies and the development of new ones); *sociocultural* (demographic trends, value systems, and market-specific beliefs and behavior); *regulatory* (import/export tariffs, taxes, product specifications, pricing and advertising policies, and patent and trademark protection); and *physical* (natural resources, climate, and health conditions) environment of the identified target market.

Value Proposition

The value proposition defines the value that an offering aims to create for target customers, the company, and its collaborators. Accordingly, when developing market offerings, a manager needs to consider three value propositions: one defining the value for target customers, one defining the value for company collaborators, and one defining the value for the company.

- The **customer value proposition** defines the benefits and associated costs that the company's offering aims to create for target customers. The customer value proposition answers the question: *How does the offering create superior value for target customers relative to the competitive offerings?*

- The **collaborator value proposition** defines the benefits and associated costs that the offering aims to create for the company collaborators. The collaborator value proposition answers the question: *How does the offering create superior value for the company's collaborators relative to the competitive offerings?*

- The **company value proposition** defines the benefits and associated costs that the offering aims to create for the company. The company value proposition answers the question: *How does the offering create superior value for the company relative to the other options the company must forgo in order to pursue this offering?*

In addition to articulating the value proposition of the offering, most marketing plans include a *positioning statement*—a succinct summary of an offering's strategy. The positioning statement identifies three aspects of the marketing strategy: an offering's *target customers*, *frame of reference* (the reference point used by customers to evaluate the offering), and the *primary benefit* of the offering (the key source of value). The key principles of writing a positioning statement are presented in Appendix B.

Tactics

The tactics section of the marketing plan outlines the means employed to translate the desired strategy into a specific set of actions. The tactical aspects of an offering—also referred to as the *marketing mix*—includes the following seven attributes: *product, service, brand, price, incentives, communication,* and *distribution*. These marketing tactics are discussed in more detail below and illustrated in Section 5 in Chapters 4–6.

- **Product.** The product section of the marketing plan captures the key product aspects of the offering, including performance, consistency, reliability, durability, compatibility, ease of use, technological design, degree of customization, form, style, and packaging. Product details and technical specifications are typically offered in a corresponding exhibit in the last section of the plan.

- **Service.** The service section of the marketing plan complements the product component by capturing the service aspects of the offering. It outlines the key decisions involved in service management, including product support, customer service, and personnel selection and training. The service aspect of the offering can be delineated in two different contexts: service provided to customers and service provided to collaborators.

- **Brand.** The brand section of the marketing plan defines the key aspects of the offering's brand, focusing on two brand elements: brand identifiers and brand referents. Brand identifiers are brand elements owned by the company and used to identify a company's products and services and differentiate them from the competition. Common brand identifiers are the brand name, logo, motto, character, soundmark, product design, and packaging. Brand referents are concepts that are meaningful to target customers and that the company aims to associate with its brand in order to enhance the customer value of the brand.

- **Price.** The price section of the marketing plan defines the monetary aspects of the offering. An offering's price is typically defined by two key components: (1) retail price—the price at which the offering is likely to be sold to end users—and (2) trade price—the price(s) at which the offering is sold to channel members, such as wholesalers, distributors, and retailers.

- **Incentives.** The incentives section of the marketing plan defines the additional, typically short-term, benefits that aim to enhance the value of the offering. An offering can involve three types of incentives: *customer incentives* such as coupons, rebates, price reductions, volume discounts, premiums, rewards, and sweepstakes; *collaborator incentives* such as advertising, slotting, stocking, display, market-development allowances, volume discounts, volume rebates, off-invoice incentives, cash discounts, financing, contests, bonus merchandise, buyback guarantees, and sales support and training; and *company incentives* such as monetary and nonmonetary bonuses, recognition awards, and contests.

- **Communication.** The communication section of the marketing plan delineates the activities that aim to inform target customers about the availability of the offering and highlight its benefits. A company's communication activities are typically guided by a communication plan (see Appendix C for an illustration of the organization of a communication plan).

- **Distribution.** The distribution section of the marketing plan delineates the channels through which the offering will be delivered from the manufacturer to end users. This section typically includes factors such as channel structure (online, brick-and-mortar, or hybrid), channel type (specialized or broad), channel coverage (extensive or limited), and channel exclusivity (exclusive or non-exclusive).

Implementation

The development of the strategic and tactical aspects of an offering is followed by defining an implementation plan that delineates the specific activities involved in executing an offering's strategy and tactics. The implementation plan involves three key components: *resource development*, *offering development*, and *commercial deployment*. These three aspects of the implementation plan are presented in more detail below and illustrated in Section 6 in Chapters 4–6.

- **Resource development.** The resource development section of the marketing plan outlines the company's efforts to secure the assets necessary to implement the company's strategy and tactics. Resource development can involve creating *business facilities* that include assets such as manufacturing, service, and information technology; creating the *organizational infrastructure* that defines the relationships among different entities within the company; ensuring reliable *suppliers*; recruiting, training, and retaining *skilled employees*; developing relevant *products*, *services*, and *brands* that can serve as a platform for the new offering; acquiring the *know-how* needed to develop, produce, and manage the offering; developing *communication* and *distribution* channels to inform target customers about the company's offering and deliver this offering to them; and securing the *capital* necessary to develop these resources.

- **Offering development.** The offering development section of the marketing plan outlines the processes that transform the company's business model into an actual good that is communicated and delivered to the company's target customers. Offering development involves managing the flow of information, materials, labor, and money in order to create the offering that the company will deploy in its target market. In addition, offering development involves designing the *product* (procurement, inbound logistics, and production) and *service* (installation, support, and repair activities); building the *brand*; setting retail and wholesale *prices* and *incentives* (coupons, rebates, and price discounts); designing the means of *communication* (message, media, and creative solution); and setting the channels of *distribution* (warehousing, order fulfillment, and transportation).

- **Commercial deployment.** The commercial deployment section of the marketing plan delineates the process of bringing the offering to the market. Commercial deployment can be selective, initially focusing on specific markets in order to assess the market reaction to the offering, or it can involve a large-scale rollout across all target markets. In cases of selective commercial deployment, the marketing plan defines the primary market in which the offering will first be introduced and outlines the key activities associated with the launch of the offering. The marketing plan further identifies the timing and the processes involved in expanding the offering beyond the primary market so that it can reach all target customers and achieve its full market potential.

Control

The control section of the marketing plan outlines the processes involved in evaluating a company's progress toward its strategic goals as well as monitoring the changes in the environment in which the company operates. The control section entails two components: *performance evaluation*, which focuses on the company's current performance, and *analysis of the environment*, which focuses on the opportunities and threats in the environment in which the company operates. The two aspects of marketing controls are discussed in more detail below and illustrated in Section 7 in Chapters 4–6.

Performance Evaluation

Performance evaluation involves evaluating the outcomes of the company's actions vis-à-vis its goals. Performance evaluation can lead to one of two outcomes: *adequate goal progress* or *performance gaps*.

- **Adequate goal progress** shows that the company is on track to achieving its goal(s).
- **Performance gaps** signify a discrepancy between the desired and actual performance on a key metric such as net income, sales revenues, or market share. To illustrate, a performance gap might involve a discrepancy between the company's desire to strengthen its market position and an actual decrease in market share.

In cases when performance evaluation reveals a gap, the current action plan needs to be modified in a way that puts the company back on track toward achieving its goal. The key principle in modifying a company's action plan is that the changes should be directly linked to the cause of the performance gap. Thus, if the primary cause of the company's inability to achieve its goals is that these goals are unrealistic, then the solution is to set new and more realistic goals. If the primary cause is inefficient strategy, then the company must reset the existing strategy—for example, by identifying new target markets, by improving the value proposition of the offering for its customers, or by introducing a new offering. Similarly, if the problem involves the offering's tactics, then the solution is to improve the offering's marketing mix—for example, by improving the product, by strengthening the brand, or by lowering the price. If the cause of the problem is poor implementation, then the company must improve the processes of developing and deploying the offering. Finally, if the cause of the problem is the use of inadequate controls, then the company should develop adequate measurements to evaluate its goal progress.

Performance can be evaluated on a variety of metrics, such as net income, market share, and unit sales. An overview of the commonly used performance metrics is offered in Appendix E.

Analysis of the Environment

The analysis of the environment aims to identify changes in the market in which the company operates and, when necessary, adjust the company's current action plan. Depending on their impact on the company, most of the market changes can be viewed as either *opportunities* or *threats*.

- **Opportunities** are factors that are likely to have a favorable impact on the company's offering. Common opportunities include improving economic conditions, the introduction of favorable government regulations, a decrease in competition, or an increase in consumer demand.

- **Threats** are factors that are likely to have an unfavorable impact on the company's offering. Common threats include declining economic conditions, the introduction of unfavorable government regulations, an increase in competition, or a decline in consumer demand.

Once a relevant change in the market conditions—an opportunity or a threat—has been identified, a company should reevaluate its current marketing plan and, when necessary, modify it to address the identified opportunities and threats. To illustrate, a company may respond to a decline in the overall economic conditions by lowering its prices and introducing sales promotions in order to continue creating superior customer value.

Exhibits

Exhibits typically make up the last section of the marketing plan. They support the analysis and the resulting course of action outlined in the marketing plan. Exhibits vary in the function they fulfill in the marketing plan and their presentation format. Based on their function, most exhibits can be classified into one of the following four categories: *market data exhibits*, *value analysis exhibits*, *offering exhibits*, and *implementation exhibits*.

- **Market data exhibits** provide additional information about the key aspects of the potential market for the company's offering: target customers (e.g., demographics, geographic location, and buying power); company (e.g., organizational structure, core competencies, and strategic assets); collaborators (e.g., firmographics, buying behavior, and strategic importance to the company); competitors (e.g., specialization, competitive intensity, and strategic alliances); and context (e.g., key regulations, technology trends, and relevant sociocultural factors).

- **Value analysis exhibits** provide information about the key aspects of the value exchange: customer value (e.g., cost–benefit analysis); collaborator value (e.g., cost–benefit analysis, margin analysis); and company value (e.g., break-even analysis, margin analysis, best-/worst-case scenario analysis).

- **Offering exhibits** provide information about the key aspects of the market offering, including product (e.g., product features and functionality); service (e.g., service specifications); brand (e.g., logo design and brand identity); price (e.g., pricing schedules); incentives (e.g., discount schedules); communication (e.g., target audiences and media allocation); and distribution (e.g., distribution coverage).

- **Implementation exhibits** provide information about the processes involved in implementing the company's offering, such as the logistics of developing the necessary resources, developing the market offering, and the commercial deployment of the offering.

The general guidelines in developing the content of the exhibits, different exhibit formats, and key principles for organizing meaningful exhibits are outlined in Appendix D.

Developing Marketing Plans for New and Existing Offerings

Marketing plans vary in the type of offerings they involve: Some plans focus on the introduction of *new offerings*, whereas others focus on managing *existing offerings* that are already available in the market.

- **New-offering plans** set a goal and develop a course of action to achieve that goal by launching a new product or service. Marketing plans for new offerings focus on evaluating the environment in which the company competes to uncover opportunities and threats and developing a course of action that takes advantage of identified opportunities and mitigates impending threats.

- **Existing-offering plans** focus on evaluating the goal progress of an existing offering and, when necessary, revising the goal and modifying the current course of action. A common example of marketing plans for managing an existing offering are a company's quarterly and annual plans.

New-offering plans and plans for managing existing offerings share many similarities. Both follow the same structure: executive summary, situation overview, goal, strategy, tactics, implementation, control, and exhibits. The key difference between these two types of plans is their focus. New-offering plans focus on *evaluating the environment* in which the company operates and *developing* a course of action to achieve company goals. In contrast, plans for managing existing offerings focus on *evaluating the changes in the environment* in which the company operates and *modifying* the current course of action, and when necessary, revising the company's goal.

Most often, the need to revise a company's marketing plan stems from a change in the circumstances in which the company operates. Such catalysts can involve a gap between the company's desired and actual performance and/or a change in the external environment that presents the company with new opportunities or threats. As a result, the changes in a company's current course of action directly follow from the change in the circumstances identified in the situation overview section of the marketing plan. For example, if the situation overview identifies a performance gap reflected in the company's loss of market share due to inferior product quality, then the action plan should include a solution to improve product quality. In the same vein, if the situation overview identifies an opportunity in the form of an emerging market segment whose needs are currently unmet by any competitors, then the action plan might involve launching a new offering targeting these customers.

PART TWO

SAMPLE MARKETING PLANS

INTRODUCTION

This section presents three stylized examples to illustrate the process of writing a marketing plan. The marketing plans presented in Chapters 4–6 follow the structure outlined earlier in this book: They begin with an *executive summary*, followed by a *situation overview* and an *action plan*, and conclude with a set of relevant *exhibits*.

The crux of the marketing plan is the action plan, which follows the G-STIC framework. It includes an outline of the *goal(s)* that identify the company's focus and the performance benchmarks to be achieved; an outline of the offering's *strategy*, which involves identifying the target market(s)—customers, the company, collaborators, competitors, and the context in which they operate—as well as the offering's value proposition for target customers, the company, and collaborators; a description of the marketing *tactics* (product, service, brand, price, incentives, communication, and distribution); an *implementation* plan that identifies the processes by which the company will develop the offering and deploy it in the market; and the *control* measures that provide the metrics for evaluating the company's performance and analyzing the external environment.

The marketing plans laid out in Chapters 4–6 involve two companies: Align Technology and DeWalt Industrial Tool Company (a division of Black & Decker).

- **Chapter 4** presents a marketing plan for launching a new offering, using the example of *Align Technology*—a startup with a proprietary method for treating the misalignment of teeth.

- **Chapter 5** presents a marketing plan for managing an existing offering. This plan builds on the *Align Technology* example shown in Chapter 4 to facilitate the comparison between marketing plans for developing new offerings and managing existing ones.

- **Chapter 6** presents a marketing plan for managing an existing offering when a company decides to make a major change in its strategy by repositioning an existing offering (discontinuing its current offering and launching a new one). This marketing plan involves *Black & Decker*—one of the world's largest power tool manufacturers—and its decision to launch a new company *DeWalt Industrial Tool Company*.

Because their primary goal is to highlight the organization of the marketing plan, the examples presented in this section are not comprehensive and do not cover all aspects of the offering in detail. Rather, they aim to illustrate the overall structure of the marketing plan and highlight its key components.

CHAPTER FOUR

SAMPLE MARKETING PLAN: ALIGN TECHNOLOGY (A)

The sample marketing plan outlined in this chapter is based on the case of Align Technology Inc.—a startup with a proprietary method for treating the misalignment of teeth. The company was born from the simple observation that dental retainers commonly prescribed after orthodontic procedures could be used not only to prevent teeth from moving but also to realign teeth. This observation led to the idea that a series of custom-designed aligners could be used to straighten misaligned teeth.

Launched in 1997 by two MBA students with no professional experience in the field of orthodontics or dentistry, the company raised more than $140 million in private capital prior to going public in January 2001. The first round of financing was led by the Menlo Park, California-based venture capital firm Kleiner Perkins Caufield & Byers, an early investor in more than 300 technology startups, including Amazon.com, Compaq, Google, Netscape, and Sun Microsystems.

Align Technology's marketing plan demonstrates the importance of understanding and managing value for each of the three key players in the market: the company, its customers, and collaborators. In addition, this marketing plan illustrates a business model that combines both business-to-business (B2B) and business-to-consumer (B2C) components. Another factor that makes this market plan particularly relevant is that it not only illustrates decisions concerning all of the key marketing mix variables (product, service, brand, price, incentives, communication, and distribution) but also highlights the relationship among them. Finally, Align's marketing plan illustrates the launch of a new-to-the-world offering.

The marketing plan for launching Align Technology's offering is delineated in the following sections. To better illustrate the relationship among the different elements of the marketing plan, the purpose of each section and the links between different sections of the marketing plan are highlighted in the sidebar.

MARKETING PLAN
ALIGN TECHNOLOGY INC.[3]

1. Executive Summary

Align Technology Inc. designs, manufactures, and markets the Invisalign system, a new proprietary method for treating malocclusion, or the misalignment of teeth. The Invisalign system corrects malocclusion using a series of clear, removable appliances that gently move teeth to a desired final position.

Our target customers are adults and adolescents with mature dentition who suffer from mild forms of malocclusion. This target group consists of approximately 65 million potential customers.

For customers, the Invisalign system offers superior aesthetics, improved dental health, and greater overall convenience relative to conventional braces. For orthodontists, the Invisalign system offers increased patient volume, higher margins, and reduced chair time compared to conventional braces. Because it offers a unique set of benefits, we believe that the Invisalign system will be well received by both orthodontists and consumers and will rapidly gain acceptance as the preferred method for treating malocclusion.

Our *primary goal* is to create value for our stakeholders by establishing the Invisalign system as the standard method for treating malocclusion. We plan to turn a profit within three years of launching the Invisalign system.

This plan outlines our key marketing activities for the period January 1999 – December 2000. Following successful implementation of this plan, we intend to take the company public in early 2001.

> The executive summary in Section 1 offers a succinct overview of the key aspects of the offering.

2. Situation Overview

Malocclusion (misalignment of teeth) is one of the most prevalent clinical conditions in the United States, affecting more than 200 million individuals, or approximately 75% of the population. Of those, approximately two million annually elect orthodontic treatment. Only a relatively small proportion of people with malocclusion seek treatment because of the compromised aesthetics, discomfort, and other drawbacks associated with conventional orthodontic treatments.

Individuals who elect to be treated for malocclusion are interacting with two entities: (1) general-practice dentists, who typically diagnose the problem and provide a referral to a specialist; and (2) orthodontists who specialize in treating malocclusion.

- *General-practice dentists* are certified to perform all oral health procedures, including orthodontics. Many general dentists, however, choose not to perform orthodontic procedures because of their complexity and the added risk of malpractice liability. There are more than 100,000 general-practice dentists in the United States.

> Section 2 offers the background information on the market in which Align Technology operates. The situation overview offered in Section 2 is broader in scope than the description of the target market offered in Section 4.1, as it includes an overview of the entire market (including markets that are not targeted by the company).

- *Orthodontists* specialize in treating malocclusions. Only board-certified orthodontists can refer to themselves as orthodontists. This certification typically involves a two-year residency after dental school. There are approximately 8,500 orthodontists in the United States.

The providers of orthodontic services apply traditional techniques and principles of treatment developed in the early 20th century. In the United States, orthodontists treat malocclusion primarily with metal archwires and brackets, commonly referred to as braces. To improve treatment aesthetics, orthodontists occasionally use ceramic, tooth-colored brackets or bond brackets on the inside, or lingual surfaces, of the patient's teeth.

The average treatment takes approximately two years to complete and requires several hours of direct orthodontist involvement, or chair time. To initiate treatment, an orthodontist will diagnose a patient's condition and create an appropriate treatment plan. In a subsequent visit, the orthodontist will bond brackets to the patient's teeth with cement and attach an archwire to the brackets. Thereafter, by tightening or otherwise adjusting the braces approximately every six weeks, the orthodontist is able to exert sufficient force on the patient's teeth to achieve desired tooth movement. Because of the length of time between visits, the orthodontist must tighten the braces to a degree sufficient to achieve sustained tooth movement during the interval. In a final visit, the orthodontist removes each bracket and residual cement from the patient's teeth.

Although braces are generally effective in correcting a wide range of malocclusions, they have many drawbacks, such as:

- *Unattractive appearance.* Braces are not visually appealing and often trap food, which further compromises appearance. Braces can also result in permanent markings and discoloration of teeth. In addition, many adults associate braces with adolescence.

- *Oral discomfort.* Braces are sharp and bulky. They can abrade and irritate the interior surfaces of the mouth. The tightening of braces during treatment results in root and gum soreness and discomfort.

- *Poor oral hygiene.* Braces compromise oral hygiene by making it more difficult to brush and floss, often resulting in tooth decay and periodontal damage.

- *Root resorption.* The sustained high levels of force associated with conventional treatment can result in root resorption, a shortening of tooth roots. This shortening can have substantial adverse periodontal consequences for the patient.

- *Emergencies.* At times, braces need to be repaired or replaced on an emergency basis. Such emergencies cause significant inconvenience to both the patient and the orthodontist.

- *Inability to project treatment.* The lack of a means to model the movement of teeth over the course of treatment limits the or-

The shortcomings of the traditional methods for treating malocclusion are later used to develop Invisalign's value proposition for target customers and collaborators (orthodontists).

thodontist's ability to estimate its duration. Because most orthodontic treatment is performed on a fixed-price basis, extended treatment duration reduces profitability for the orthodontist.

- *Physical demands on orthodontists.* The manipulation of wires and brackets requires sustained manual dexterity and visual acuity from the orthodontist.

Fees for orthodontic treatment typically range between $3,000 and $5,000. Orthodontists also commonly charge a premium for the more aesthetically appealing lingual or ceramic alternatives. Fees are based on the difficulty of the particular case and on the orthodontist's estimate of chair time and are generally negotiated in advance. Treatment that exceeds the orthodontist's estimate of chair time is typically covered by the orthodontist at no additional charge. Most insurance plans do not cover orthodontic treatments for adults and offer limited coverage for children and adolescents.

3. Goal

Our *primary goal* is to create value for our shareholders by establishing the Invisalign system as the standard method for treating malocclusion. We plan to turn a profit within three years of launching Invisalign.

To achieve our primary goal, we have set the following objectives:

- *Customer objectives.* Our key customer objectives are to create awareness of the benefits of the Invisalign system among 20% of our target customers, stimulate their interest, and incite action leading to treatment using the Invisalign system. Our goal is to have 50,000 patients initiate treatment with the Invisalign system by the end of 2001.

- *Collaborator objectives.* We aim to create awareness of the benefits of the Invisalign system among orthodontists, train them to use the system, and motivate them to promote it to patients as the standard method for treating malocclusion. Our goal is to create awareness among 90% of orthodontists and train 2,000 of them to use the Invisalign system by the end of 2001.

- *Internal objectives.* We strive to constantly improve the proprietary technology that underlies our supply-chain management processes to enhance product quality, increase production capacity, and reduce both unit costs and production times.

- *Competitive objectives.* Our primary competitive objective is to create barriers to entry for competitors. We will pursue further intellectual property protection through patent applications and nondisclosure agreements. We also seek to protect our proprietary technology under trade secret and copyright laws.

Section 3 outlines the company's primary goal as well as a series of objectives focusing on customers, collaborators, the company, and competitors.

4. Strategy

4.1. Target Market

Customers

Based on the degree to which individuals suffering from malocclusion have developed dentition, they can be divided into two groups: (1) children/adolescents whose teeth/jaws are still developing and (2) adolescents/adults with mature dentition.

Our target customers are adults and adolescents with mature dentition who suffer from malocclusion and are otherwise suitable for treatment using the Invisalign system. This group represents approximately 65 million potential customers. Although we have clearance from the FDA to market the Invisalign system to treat patients with any type of malocclusion, we voluntarily restrict the use of the Invisalign system to adults and adolescents with mature dentition who are otherwise suitable for treatment. Accordingly, we will not treat children whose teeth and jaws are still developing, as the effectiveness of the Invisalign system relies on our ability to accurately predict the movement of teeth over the course of treatment.

Our research indicates that, based on the primary reason for treatment, there are two groups of customers: *health conscious* and *appearance conscious*. Health-conscious consumers are primarily concerned with strengthening their teeth for health reasons and are less concerned about their appearance during treatment. In contrast, appearance-conscious consumers are concerned about their appearance and might not elect to undergo orthodontic treatment if it will affect their appearance during treatment.

These two segments are likely to differ in their preference for a treatment method. Because their primary concern is the health of their teeth, health-conscious consumers tend to rely on orthodontists' recommendations for choosing the treatment method (traditional braces vs. Invisalign). In contrast, appearance-conscious consumers are likely to approach orthodontists with a specific request for Invisalign treatment. Health-conscious and appearance-conscious consumers are also likely to differ in their decision-making process. Health-conscious consumers first visit an orthodontist and only then select a treatment, usually following the orthodontist's recommendation. In contrast, appearance-conscious consumers are likely to choose Invisalign as their treatment method of choice based on Invisalign advertisements prior to visiting an orthodontist. Exhibit 1 provides detailed information on the customer survey.

Collaborators

Our primary collaborators are US-based licensed orthodontists. We expect orthodontists to contribute to the success of the Invisalign system by (1) informing patients about the availability and benefits of the Invisalign system, (2) implementing the Invisalign treatment,

---

Section 4.1 follows the 5-C framework.

This section identifies the offering's target customers.

Note that the targeting decision involves not only target customers, but also those who are not targeted.

This section further identifies two different target segments that are likely to vary in their response to the Invisalign system. The segmentation of customers into appearance-conscious and health-conscious is later used to develop a segment-specific marketing mix, using a pull strategy for appearance-conscious consumers and a push strategy for health-conscious consumers.

This section identifies the key collaborators that will facilitate the success of the Invisalign system.

and (3) providing performance feedback that will enable us to improve the Invisalign system.

The Invisalign system will be available only to orthodontists. Although dentists play an important role in informing patients about orthodontics and are a key source of referrals to orthodontists, the Invisalign system will not be available to general dentists.

Competitors

As a new technique for treating malocclusion, Align Technology does not have direct competitors and currently competes with the traditional techniques to treat malocclusion, the most common of which is metal braces. In the broader market for orthodontic products that treat malocclusion, we are indirectly competing with 3M Company, Sybron International Corporation, and Dentsply International, Inc.

The positioning statement identifies the key competitors and evaluates the current and future competitive intensity of the marketplace.

We are not aware of any company that has developed or is marketing a system comparable to the Invisalign system. Because the availability of the Invisalign system is likely to generate new demand by attracting appearance-conscious consumers who would not otherwise choose an orthodontic treatment, we do not expect an immediate response from the manufacturers of traditional orthodontic products for malocclusion. However, over time we expect the competition in this segment to increase with the emergence of new competitors with similar products.

Company

Align Technology Inc. was incorporated in Delaware in 1997. The corporate headquarters are located in Santa Clara, California, where we house our manufacturing, customer support, software engineering, and administrative personnel. We also operate two facilities in the city of Lahore in Pakistan.

This section provides general information about the company.

We currently have 320 employees, of whom 120 are employed in the United States, with the balance employed in Pakistan. Our organizational structure is outlined in Exhibit 2. Our management consists of (1) executive officers, (2) scientific advisory board, and (3) board of directors (listed in Exhibits 3–5). We are currently building specialized production facilities, creating a network of orthodontists trained to use the Invisalign system, building brand recognition, and creating an initial customer base.

Our core competency is producing highly customized, close tolerance, medical-quality products in volume. Our strategic assets include intellectual property (proprietary technology with pending patent application), manufacturing infrastructure, and the Invisalign and ClinCheck brands.

Context

Economic context: Continuous economic growth for seven consecutive years, low unemployment, high consumer confidence, low interest rates, and low inflation. Stock market powered by gains in technology stocks and a record number of technology-based IPOs.

This section outlines the context in which Align Technology operates.

Regulatory context: Laws regulating medical device manufacturers and health care providers cover a broad array of subjects, including:

- The confidentiality of patient medical information and the circumstances under which such information may be released for inclusion in our databases, or released by us to third parties, are subject to substantial regulation by state governments.

- Federal and state regulations prohibit paying any remuneration in exchange for the referral of patients to a person participating in federal or state healthcare programs, such as Medicare and Medicaid.

- Various states regulate the operation of an advertising and referral service for dentists and may require compliance with various requirements on how they structure their relationships with participating dentists.

- According to the FDA classification of medical devices, the Invisalign system is a Class I device, the least stringent class, that does not require a premarket approval, which includes, among other things, extensive preclinical and clinical trials.

4.2. Customer Value Proposition

Value Proposition

There is an unmet need among our target customers for a malocclusion treatment that eliminates many of the limitations of conventional braces. Test market data presented in Exhibit 6 show that the Invisalign system offers a number of unique benefits to our target customers:

This section outlines the key benefits of the Invisalign system for target customers. It answers the question: Why would target customers opt to straighten their teeth using the Invisalign system?

- *Excellent aesthetics.* Aligners are nearly invisible when worn, eliminating the aesthetic concerns associated with conventional braces.

- *Improved oral hygiene.* Patients can remove Aligners when eating, brushing, and flossing, a feature that can reduce tooth decay and periodontal damage during treatment.

- *Greater safety.* By replacing the six-week adjustment cycle of traditional braces with two-week stages, the Invisalign system moves teeth more gently, decreasing the likelihood of root resorption (shortening of tooth roots).

- *Increased comfort.* The Invisalign system is substantially more comfortable and less abrasive than conventional braces.

- *Reduced overall treatment time.* The Invisalign system controls force by distributing it broadly over the exposed surfaces of the teeth while at the same time reducing the likelihood of unintended tooth movements. This could significantly reduce overall treatment time relative to conventional braces.

- *Reduced incidence of emergencies.* Lost or broken Aligners could be simply replaced with the next Aligner in the series, minimizing inconvenience to both patient and orthodontist.

Positioning Statement

For adults and adolescents with mild forms of malocclusion, In-visalign is a better treatment than conventional braces because it of-fers superior aesthetics, improved dental health, and greater overall convenience.

This section identifies target customers and the key benefits of the In-visalign system.

4.3. Collaborator Value Proposition

Value Proposition

The Invisalign system offers the following benefits to orthodontists:

This section outlines the key benefits of the In-visalign system for or-thodontists. It answers the question: *Why would orthodontists opt to use the Invisalign system instead of conventional braces?*

- *Ability to visualize treatment and likely outcomes.* The Invisalign system enables orthodontists to preview a course of treatment and the likely final outcome of treatment in an interactive three-dimensional computer model. This allows orthodontists to analyze multiple treatment alternatives before selecting the one most appropriate for the patient.

- *Ability to predict treatment time.* Because patient fees are based on the orthodontist's estimate of chair time and are generally negotiated in advance, treatment that exceeds the orthodon-tist's estimate of chair time is typically covered by the ortho-dontist at no additional charge. By improving the accuracy of the estimate of treatment time, Invisalign can help orthodon-tists better manage resources and optimize profits.

- *Ease of use.* Because the Invisalign system relies on the same bio-mechanical principles that underlie traditional orthodontic treat-ment, it is straightforward for orthodontists to learn and to use. The initial certification training can be completed in a one-day workshop, and orthodontists can be equipped to submit cases immediately thereafter with minimal financial outlay.

- *Increased patient base.* Currently, less than one percent of the more than 200 million people with malocclusion in the United States enter treatment each year. The Invisalign system allows orthodontists to broaden their patient base by offering a new, attractive treatment alternative to people who would not oth-erwise elect treatment.

- *Higher margins.* The Invisalign system enables orthodontists to more accurately estimate the duration of the treatment, thus decreasing the likelihood of underestimating the treatment length and increasing the overall profit margins per patient. Due to the substantial benefits to customers, orthodontists can also charge a premium for the Invisalign system comparable to other more aesthetically pleasing alternatives to conventional braces, such as ceramic and lingual braces.

- *Decreased orthodontist and staff time.* The Invisalign system re-duces both the frequency and length of patient visits. It elimi-nates the need for time-intensive processes, such as bonding appliances to the patient's teeth, adjusting archwires during the course of treatment, and removing the appliances at the conclusion of treatment. As a result, use of the Invisalign system significantly reduces orthodontist and staff chair time and can increase practice throughput.

Positioning Statement

For orthodontists, the Invisalign system is a better method for treating most cases of malocclusion than conventional braces because it offers increased patient volume, higher margins, and reduced chair time.

4.4. Company Value Proposition

Value Proposition

Align Technology earns revenue primarily from the sale of our Invisalign system, which consists of the ClinCheck fee and a per-Aligner fee. Our per-customer revenue is $1,180 and our per-customer gross profit is $875. With a market potential of 65 million customers, this implies potential sales revenues as high as $75 billion.

Currently, we are the only company with a commercially available alternative to conventional braces. As our business grows, new competitors are likely to enter the market. The inherent complexity of producing highly customized, high-precision orthodontic devices in volume is a barrier to potential competitors. We further believe that our patents and other intellectual property provide a substantial lead over potential competitors. Therefore, we believe that our business model is sustainable and can offer long-term value to shareholders.

Due to our national advertising campaign, the expansion of manufacturing capacity, and continued research-and-development efforts, we expect to incur net losses for the next several years. We plan to turn a profit within three years of launching Invisalign sales. Detailed financial information and the key assumptions are provided in Exhibits 7–8.

Positioning Statement

To investors who are interested in investing in a startup company with a high growth potential, Align Technology offers an opportunity to pioneer a $75 billion market for orthodontic devices with a patented system that offers unique benefits to both patients and orthodontists.

Executive Compensation

Compensation schedules for our executive officers, scientific advisory board, and board of directors, as well as the composition of the executive compensation committee are disclosed in Exhibit 9.

Employee Compensation

Our full-time employees (excluding the sales force) are compensated in two ways: salary and stock options. Salaries are competitive with the high end of comparable positions within the industry. The stock options are based on seniority with the company. We also offer

---

Sidebar notes:

This section identifies the company's collaborators and the key benefits of the Invisalign system.

This section outlines the value of the offering to the company. Because the key aspects of company value are reflected in the company's goal, this section restates the goal outlined in Section 3.

This section further delineates the key benefits of the Invisalign system for stakeholders. It answers the question: *Why should stakeholders invest in Invisalign instead of pursuing other investment options?*

This section identifies the key stakeholders and the key benefits of the Invisalign system.

Employee satisfaction has a direct impact on performance and is an important component in defining an offering's value proposition.

health insurance benefits to all full-time employees, effective the day they begin work.

Sales Force Compensation

Our sales force is divided regionally and compensated on a 60 percent salary, 15 percent commission, and 25 percent bonus structure. Salaries are competitive with the high end of comparable positions within the industry. Commission is a function of the number of cases submitted and bonuses are based on nonsales objectives, such as number of workshops conducted for orthodontists. The compensation structure also includes a company car, stock options based on seniority, and full insurance benefits.

Because sales force compensation constitutes a substantial part of the overall employee expenditures and has a distinct compensation structure, it is discussed in a separate section.

5. Tactics

5.1. Product

The Invisalign system is a proprietary new method for treating malocclusion. It consists of two components: ClinCheck and Aligners.

- *ClinCheck* is an interactive Internet application that allows orthodontists to diagnose and plan treatment for their patients. ClinCheck uses a dental impression and a treatment prescription submitted by an orthodontist to develop a customized, three-dimensional treatment plan that simulates appropriate tooth movement in a series of two-week increments. ClinCheck allows the orthodontist to view this three-dimensional simulation with a high degree of magnification and from any angle.

- *Aligners* are custom-manufactured, clear, removable dental appliances that when worn in the prescribed series provide orthodontic treatment. Each Aligner covers a patient's teeth and is nearly invisible when worn. Aligners are commonly worn in pairs (over the upper and lower dental arches) for consecutive two-week periods that correspond to the approved ClinCheck treatment simulation. After two weeks of use, the patient discards the Aligners and replaces them with the next pair in the series. This process is repeated until the final Aligners are used and treatment is complete. The typical Invisalign system patient uses 22 sets of Aligners over 44 weeks of treatment. Detailed product specifications are provided in Exhibit 10.

Section 5.1 outlines the product aspect of the Invisalign system.

The ClinCheck application can also be viewed as part of the service aspect of the Invisalign system (orthodontists do not acquire the rights to the software application but merely gain the right to use it on a limited basis); however, because it is an essential component of creating the product (Aligners), it is presented as a component of the product aspect of the offering.

5.2. Service

We offer support services to orthodontists who elect to use the Invisalign system. These services include initial training, assistance with current cases, and practice-building assistance.

- *Initial training* is conducted in a workshop format by our sales and orthodontic teams. The key topics covered in training include case selection criteria, instructions on filling out the Invisalign prescription form, guidance on pricing, and instructions on interacting with the ClinCheck software and using the Invisalign website.

Section 5.2 outlines the service aspect of the Invisalign system, focusing on the service provided to orthodontists using the Invisalign system.

- *Current-case support* may include assisting orthodontists with the applicability and use of the Invisalign system for specific patients.

- *Practice-building assistance* helps orthodontists promote their services to local general-practice dentists and to prospective patients through direct mail or other media.

5.3. Brand

We use two brands to differentiate our offering: ClinCheck and Invisalign.

- *ClinCheck.* We use the brand ClinCheck in reference to the interactive Internet application that allows orthodontists to diagnose and plan treatment for their patients. We use the ClinCheck brand in our communication to orthodontists and general-practice dentists; it is not used in consumer communication. The ClinCheck name is our registered trademark.

- *Invisalign.* We use the brand Invisalign in reference to the process of straightening teeth using a series of invisible Aligners. We use the Invisalign brand in our communication to consumers, orthodontists, and general-practice dentists. We have filed applications for several relevant trademarks with the US Patent and Trademark Office, including Invisalign and Invisalign system, as well as the Invisalign system logo. Our brand identity marks are illustrated in Exhibit 11.

> Section 5.3 outlines the brands used by Align Technology to create a unique identity for its offering.
>
> Note that while both brands—ClinCheck and Invisalign—are promoted to orthodontists, only the latter is used in consumer communication.

5.4. Pricing

The price for the orthodontic treatment is negotiated by the orthodontist and the patient. We expect the average retail price for the orthodontists' services (including Aligners) to be around $5,000 to $7,000 depending on the severity of the case.

Align Technology charges orthodontists $300 for the setup fee and $20 for each Aligner. The ClinCheck fee is invoiced when the orthodontist orders ClinCheck prior to the production of Aligners. The fee for Aligners is invoiced when we ship them. The average cost of the Aligners to orthodontists is about $1,180 per patient (assuming a course of treatment consisting of 22 pairs of Aligners at $20 each and a setup fee of $300).

> Section 5.4 outlines the price of the Invisalign system for both patients and orthodontists.
>
> Note that Align Technology does not determine the retail price of the treatment, but only the price of Invisalign for orthodontists.

5.5. Incentives

We offer incentives to both our target customers and collaborators.

- *Incentives for customers.* Because the specifics and cost of the treatment are negotiated directly between the orthodontist and the patient, we are not offering direct incentives to consumers.

- *Incentives for orthodontists.* We use a system of tiering orthodontists that encourages our sales force to devote more time to those orthodontists most proficient in the use of the Invisalign system. We use objective criteria, primarily the number of cases

> Section 5.5 outlines the incentives provided to target customers and collaborators.

initiated with the Invisalign system, to tier orthodontists. Inquiries from prospective patients through our customer call center and our website are directed to higher tier orthodontists. This tiering process should incentivize the selected orthodontists, rapidly increasing the use of the Invisalign system by their offices.

- *Incentives for general-practice dentists.* We have no immediate plans to offer incentives to dentists for referring potential Invisalign patients to orthodontists.

5.6. Communication

Consumer Communication

Consumers can learn about the benefits of the Invisalign system in one of three ways: (1) directly from Align Technology, (2) from orthodontists, and/or (3) from general-practice dentists. Accordingly, we use two basic strategies to reach our target customers. We use a *pull strategy* (direct-to-consumer communication) to target appearance-conscious consumers who might not consider orthodontic treatment unless they are made aware of the existence of an aesthetically appealing malocclusion treatment. In addition, we use a *push strategy* (informing and incentivizing orthodontists) to target health-conscious consumers who rely on orthodontists' advice for the choice of treatment.

This section outlines the communication to target customers.

Note that the use of pull vs. push strategy in the case of direct vs. indirect communication directly follows from the analysis of the target market in Section 4.1.

- *Direct-to-consumer (pull) communication*
  - *Media.* We promote the Invisalign system by communicating its benefits directly to consumers with a nationwide television and radio advertising campaign. We also provide consumers with information about the Invisalign system through our toll-free phone line (1-800-INVISIBLE) and our website (invisalign.com).
  - *Message.* Because the direct-to-consumer campaign targets appearance-conscious consumers, our message will focus on the aesthetic benefits and the overall convenience of using the Invisalign system.
  - *Slogan.* Our slogan is "Clear alternative to braces."
- *Indirect (push) consumer communication.* To facilitate recommendations of the Invisalign system, we provide orthodontists and general-practice dentists with promotional materials that include brochures, calendars, and posters to be displayed in their offices and/or given to patients who express interest.

The content of the message to target customers follows directly from the value proposition and the positioning statement outlined in Section 4.2.

Additional information on our consumer communication is provided in Exhibit 12.

Collaborator Communication

Orthodontists can learn about the Invisalign system from our mass-media consumer advertising as well as from our communication targeting orthodontists.

This section outlines the communication to the company's collaborators.

- *Media*. We use print advertisements in professional press targeting orthodontists, event sponsorship for orthodontic conventions and conferences, as well as direct mail and telemarketing targeting individual orthodontic practices. In addition, we have a sales team comprising approximately 30 salespeople experienced in orthodontic product sales.

- *Message*. Our message focuses on the potential to substantially improve orthodontic practice profitability through increased patient volume, higher margins, and reduced chair time.

| The content of the message to orthodontists follows directly from the value proposition outlined in Section 4.3. |

Additional information on our communication to orthodontists is provided in Exhibit 13.

5.7. Distribution

The Invisalign system is distributed exclusively through orthodontists and is not available for retail purchase by consumers directly from Align Technology. Only orthodontists are authorized to use the Invisalign system; it is not available to general-practice dentists. Orders are processed through headquarters and shipped in batches directly to orthodontist offices from the manufacturing facilities in Mexico. The first batch includes the first several months of treatment and is manufactured once the prescribing orthodontist approves ClinCheck. Thereafter, Aligners are sent at approximately six-month intervals until treatment is complete.

| Section 5.7 outlines the distribution channel for the Invisalign system. |

6. Implementation

6.1. Resource Development

We plan to expand our operations to two facilities in Santa Clara, California, which will serve as our manufacturing headquarters. These facilities are designed to produce highly customized, medical-quality products in high volume using a number of proprietary processes and technologies. These technologies include complex software solutions, laser, destructive and white light scanning techniques and stereolithography, wax modeling, and other rapid prototyping methods.

| Section 6.1 outlines the resources necessary for implementing the marketing plan. |

The fabrication and packaging of Aligners is outsourced to a contract manufacturer based in Juarez, Mexico. The creation of treatment simulations is done in our facilities in Lahore, Pakistan. The telephone support to handle information requests and orthodontist referrals is outsourced to a large national call center operator.

Additional information on the development of our business facilities, service infrastructure, supply channels, and sales force is provided in Exhibit 14.

6.2. Developing the Invisalign System

To implement the Invisalign system we developed and tested the following five-stage process:

| Section 6.2 outlines the process of developing the Invisalign system. |

- *Orthodontic diagnosis and transmission of treatment data to Align Technology.* In an initial patient visit, the orthodontist determines whether the Invisalign system is an appropriate treatment. The orthodontist then prepares treatment data that consist of an impression of the dental arches, X-rays of the patient's dentition, photographs of the patient, and an Invisalign system treatment planning form, or prescription. The prescription describes the desired positions and movement of the patient's teeth. The orthodontist sends the treatment data to our Santa Clara facility.

- *Preparation of three-dimensional computer models of the patient's initial malocclusion.* On receipt, we use the treatment data to construct plaster models of the patient's dentition. We scan the plaster models to develop a digital, three-dimensional computer model of the patient's current dentition. We then transmit this initial computer model together with the orthodontist's prescription to our facilities in Lahore, Pakistan.

- *Preparation of computer-simulated treatment and viewing of treatment using ClinCheck.* In Pakistan, we transform the initial model into a customized, three-dimensional treatment plan that simulates appropriate tooth movement in a series of two-week increments. This simulation is then transmitted back to our Santa Clara facility for review. After passing review, the simulation is then delivered to the prescribing orthodontist via ClinCheck on our website. The orthodontist then reviews the ClinCheck simulation and, when necessary, asks us to make adjustments. The orthodontist then approves the proposed treatment and, in doing so, engages us for the manufacture of corresponding Aligners.

- *Construction of molds corresponding to each step of treatment.* We use the approved ClinCheck simulation to construct a series of molds of the patient's teeth. Each mold is a replica of the patient's teeth at each two-week stage of the simulated course of treatment. These molds are fabricated at our Santa Clara facility using custom manufacturing techniques that we have adapted for use in orthodontic applications.

- *Manufacturing of Aligners and shipment to orthodontist.* We ship these molds to Juarez, Mexico, where our contract manufacturer fabricates Aligners by pressure forming polymeric sheets over each mold. The Aligners are then trimmed, polished, cleaned, packaged, and, following final inspection, shipped directly to the prescribing orthodontist.

We are currently conducting clinical trials to validate and optimize this process. We expect to exit the development stage in July 2000. Additional information on developing the Invisalign offering is provided in Exhibit 15.

6.3. Commercial Deployment

Commercial sales are planned to commence in July 1999 with a national direct-to-consumer advertising campaign. During the first year, the Invisalign system would be available through a limited number of orthodontists who will help us optimize our offering to better serve the needs of the patients and orthodontists. Our commercial deployment schedule is outlined in more detail in Exhibit 16.

Section 6.3 outlines the key aspects of the commercial deployment of the Invisalign system.

7. Control

7.1. Performance Evaluation

We are constantly monitoring our financial performance to ensure that we are on track toward achieving our goals. In addition to net revenues and sales revenues reported in our financial statements, we use the following metrics to monitor our performance:

Section 7.1 outlines the key metrics used to measure the progress toward the goal defined in Section 3.

- Number of new patients initiating treatment using Invisalign products

- Number of dental professionals trained to use the Invisalign system

- Penetration rate (number of dental professionals who have adopted the Invisalign system)

We also actively solicit product-related feedback from orthodontists and general-practice dentists to improve the technology underlying the Invisalign system.

7.2. Analysis of the Environment

We are constantly monitoring for changes in the environment, including the following:

Section 7.2 outlines the process of monitoring for changes in the environment in which the company operates.

- Changes in customer preferences

- Changes in our internal resources and competencies

- Changes in the value the Invisalign system delivers to our collaborators (orthodontists and general-practice dentists)

- Changes in the competitive landscape (e.g., entrance of new competitors)

- Changes in the economic, business, sociocultural, technological, regulatory, and physical context in which the company operates

To ensure that we are aware of the potential changes in the environment, we engage in the following activities:

- Monitor the USPTO database for new patent and trademark applications

- Participate in professional conferences and trade shows

- Examine professional publications

- Conduct proprietary research to examine consumer and dental professionals' experience with our offerings
- Review secondary research dealing with new developments in orthodontic technology and marketing practices

A detailed description of the performance metrics is offered in Exhibit 17.

8. Exhibits

Exhibit 1: Consumer survey

Exhibit 2: Organizational structure

Exhibit 3: Senior management

Exhibit 4: Board of directors

Exhibit 5: Scientific advisory board

Exhibit 6: Test market data

Exhibit 7: Financial statements and projections

Exhibit 8: Key assumptions

Exhibit 9: Executive compensation

Exhibit 10: Product specifications

Exhibit 11: Brand identity

Exhibit 12: Consumer communication

Exhibit 13: Communication to orthodontists

Exhibit 14: Infrastructure development

Exhibit 15: Developing the Invisalign system

Exhibit 16: Commercial deployment

Exhibit 17: Performance metrics

Section 8 outlines documentation supporting the marketing plan (for brevity, the actual exhibits are not included in this plan).

CHAPTER FIVE

SAMPLE MARKETING PLAN: ALIGN TECHNOLOGY (B)

The marketing plan presented in this chapter builds on the marketing plan shown in the previous chapter and is written ten years after the company's launch in 1997 and six years after its IPO in 2001. Since the launch of commercial sales, the Invisalign system has been adopted by nearly 90% of the orthodontists in the United States. Many of the top dental schools have added specialized Invisalign courses to their curriculum. During the past decade, an excess of one million patients have been treated with the help of the Invisalign system.

The use of Align Technology to illustrate the content of a marketing plan for managing existing offerings allows a direct comparison with the plan presented in the previous chapter. This comparison is informative because it underscores the different decisions the company must make with respect to the marketing mix variables—including product line extensions, new service introduction, brand repositioning and brand extension, as well as changes in the pricing structure and communication. This plan also illustrates a company's transition from a single offering to a product line and defines a set of marketing metrics designed to monitor the company's performance and the external environment in which it operates.

The marketing plan outlined in this chapter follows the structure of the plan outlined in the previous chapter. The key difference is that whereas the plan presented earlier focused on defining the key aspects of the company's soon-to-be-launched offering, the plan outlined in this chapter explicitly focuses on the *changes* that need to be made to the company's current action plan. Thus, many of the sections present a number of specific changes the company intends to implement during the period covered by the marketing plan. To better illustrate the relationship between the different components of the marketing plan presented in this chapter, the purpose of each section and the links between different sections of the marketing plan are highlighted in the sidebar.

ANNUAL MARKETING PLAN
ALIGN TECHNOLOGY INC.[4]

1. Executive Summary

Align Technology Inc. designs, manufactures, and markets the Invisalign system, a proprietary method for treating malocclusion, or the misalignment of teeth. The Invisalign system corrects malocclusion using a series of clear, removable appliances that gently move teeth to a desired position. For patients, the Invisalign system offers superior aesthetics, improved dental health, and greater overall convenience relative to conventional braces. For dental professionals, the Invisalign system offers increased patient volume and higher margins compared to conventional orthodontic procedures.

Our *primary goal* is to create value for our stakeholders by establishing the Invisalign system as the standard method for treating malocclusion.

Our key *strategic initiatives* for the current planning period are:

- Continue growing our current target markets (adult consumers) in the United States and abroad.

- Expand our target market to include teenagers (age 12 and older) whose teeth are still growing.

- Increase adoption and utilization rate of Invisalign among dental professionals.

- Accelerate product and technology innovation to enhance clinical efficacy.

This plan outlines our key marketing activities for the period January 2008 – December 2008.

2. Situation Overview

Malocclusion (misalignment of teeth) is one of the most prevalent clinical conditions in the United States, affecting more than 195 million individuals, or about 65% of the population. Approximately 2.3 million people annually elect treatment by orthodontists in the United States; approximately 40% of these patients, or approximately 900,000, have mature dentition, with substantially completed teeth and jaw growth with mild to moderate malocclusions. Only a small proportion of people with malocclusion seek treatment because of the compromised aesthetics, discomfort, and other drawbacks associated with conventional orthodontic treatments.

Consumers who elect to be treated for malocclusion are interacting with two entities: (1) general-practice dentists, who typically diagnose the problem and provide a referral to a specialist; and (2) orthodontists who specialize in treating malocclusion.

- *Dentists*. General dentists are certified to perform all oral health procedures, including orthodontics. Many general dentists,

---

The executive summary in Section 1 offers a succinct overview of the key aspects of the offering, its goal, and key strategic initiatives.

Section 2 offers the background information on the market in which Align Technology operates. The market overview offered here is broader in scope than the description of the target market offered in Section 4.1 as it includes an overview of the entire market (including markets that are not targeted by the company).

The market overview section also delineates the

however, choose not to perform specialized procedures, such as periodontics, prosthodontics, and orthodontics, because of their complexity and the added risk of malpractice liability. There are more than 100,000 general-practice dentists in the United States.

- *Orthodontists.* Orthodontists specialize in treating malocclusions. Only board-certified orthodontists can refer to themselves as orthodontists. This certification typically involves a two-year residency after dental school. There are approximately 10,500 orthodontists in the United States.

Malocclusion is traditionally treated with metal archwires and brackets, commonly referred to as braces. To improve treatment aesthetics, orthodontists occasionally use ceramic, tooth-colored brackets, or bond brackets on the inside, or lingual surfaces, of the patient's teeth.

The average treatment takes approximately two years to complete and requires several hours of direct orthodontist involvement, or chair time. To initiate treatment, an orthodontist will diagnose a patient's condition and create an appropriate treatment plan. In a subsequent visit, the orthodontist will bond brackets to the patient's teeth with cement and attach an archwire to the brackets. Thereafter, by tightening or otherwise adjusting the braces approximately every six weeks, the orthodontist is able to exert sufficient force on the patient's teeth to achieve desired tooth movement. Because of the length of time between visits, the orthodontist must tighten the braces to a degree sufficient to achieve sustained tooth movement during the interval. In a final visit, the orthodontist removes each bracket and residual cement from the patient's teeth.

Although braces are generally effective in correcting a wide range of malocclusions, they have many drawbacks, such as:

- *Unattractive appearance.* Braces are visually unattractive and often trap food, which further compromises appearance. Braces can also result in permanent marks and discoloration of teeth. In addition, many adults associate braces with adolescence.

- *Oral discomfort.* Braces are sharp and bulky. They can abrade and irritate the interior surfaces of the mouth. The tightening of braces during treatment results in root and gum soreness and discomfort.

- *Poor oral hygiene.* Braces compromise oral hygiene by making it more difficult to brush and floss, often resulting in tooth decay and periodontal damage.

- *Root resorption.* The sustained high levels of force associated with conventional treatment can result in root resorption, a shortening of tooth roots. This shortening can have substantial adverse periodontal consequences for the patient.

- *Emergencies.* At times, braces need to be repaired or replaced on an emergency basis. Such emergencies cause significant inconvenience to both the patient and the orthodontist.

key changes in the market and outlines the progress achieved by Align Technology.

- *Inability to project treatment.* The lack of a means to model the movement of teeth over a course of treatment limits the orthodontist's ability to estimate its duration. Because most orthodontic treatment is performed on a fixed price basis, extended treatment duration reduces profitability for the orthodontist.

- *Physical demands on orthodontists.* The manipulation of wires and brackets requires sustained manual dexterity and visual acuity from the orthodontist.

Fees for orthodontic treatment typically range between \$3,500 and \$7,000, with a median fee of approximately \$5,000. Orthodontists also commonly charge a premium for the more aesthetically appealing lingual or ceramic alternatives. Fees are based on the difficulty of the particular case and on the orthodontist's estimate of chair time and are generally negotiated in advance. Treatment that exceeds the orthodontist's estimate of chair time is typically covered by the orthodontist at no additional charge. Most insurance plans do not cover orthodontic treatments for adults and offer limited coverage for children and adolescents.

So far, approximately 732,000 patients worldwide have started treatment using Invisalign. The Invisalign system is sold in North America, Europe, Asia-Pacific, Latin America, and Japan. We have trained over 48,000 dental professionals worldwide. The Invisalign technique has been incorporated into the curriculum of 63 university programs worldwide. In 2002, Invisalign was made available to general practitioner dentists and in mid-2003, leading dental schools began adding Invisalign to their curriculum.

In 2005, Align introduced Invisalign Express (now Invisalign Express 10), a lower priced solution for less complex orthodontic cases, launched Invisalign in Japan, and achieved a manufacturing milestone of 15 million unique clear aligners. In 2007, Align added distribution partners in Asia-Pacific and Latin America, and introduced Vivera® retainers.

At the beginning of 2008, our product line includes two offerings: Invisalign Full, our flagship product, and Invisalign Express, a shorter duration solution for minor cases. Approximately 88% of our net revenues are generated by the sale of Invisalign Full and 8% are generated by the sale of Invisalign Express.

3. Goal

Our *primary goal* is to create value for our stakeholders by establishing the Invisalign system as the standard method for treating malocclusion. In particular, we aim to increase our revenue by 10% to \$300 million, our gross margins from 73.6% to 75%, and our operating margins from 12.5% to 14%. To achieve this goal, we have set the following objectives:

- *Customer objectives.* Our key customer objectives are to create awareness of the benefits of the Invisalign system among 90% of our target customers, stimulate their interest, and generate new demand for our Invisalign offerings. We aim to have

Section 3 outlines the company's primary goal, as well as the specific customer, collaborator, company, and competitor objectives.

200,000 patients initiate treatment with the Invisalign system in 2008.

- *Collaborator objectives.* We aim to create awareness of the benefits of the Invisalign system among dental professionals, train them to use the system, and motivate them to promote it to patients as the standard method for treating malocclusion. Our goal is to train 500 new orthodontists and 5,000 new general-practice dentists in the United States, and 2,000 dental professionals in Europe, our primary international market. In addition, we aim to increase the frequency of using the Invisalign system (utilization rate) per participating dental professional by 10%.

- *Internal objectives.* Accelerate product and technology innovation, while at the same time extend clinical efficacy. Streamline our supply-chain management processes to enhance product quality, increase production capacity, and reduce both unit costs and production times.

- *Competitive objectives.* Our primary competitive objective is to further differentiate our offerings from those offered by our competitors, while continuing to create barriers to entry for competitors. We will pursue further intellectual property protection through patent applications and nondisclosure agreements under trade secret and copyright laws.

4. Strategy

4.1. Target Market

Section 4.1 follows the 5-C framework.

Customers

Our current target market are *adults and adolescents with mature dentition* who are otherwise suitable for treatment. Our share is approximately 8% of the 900,000 patients with mature dentition who annually elect to seek orthodontic treatment. So far, we have elected not to treat children whose teeth and jaws are still developing because of our limited ability to accurately predict the movement of teeth during the course of treatment.

This section identifies the offering's target customers. It summarizes the key aspects of the target segment outlined in Section 3.3, providing a more detailed analysis of target customers.

In 2008 we plan to expand our target market to include teenagers (age 12 and older) whose teeth are still growing, a move facilitated by the advances in technology that enable us to accurately control the movement of teeth over the course of treatment even for patients whose teeth are still growing.

Geographically, our target markets include the United States, Europe, Canada, Mexico, Brazil, Australia, Hong Kong, and Japan. We are not planning to expand into new markets in 2008.

Collaborators

Our primary collaborators are dental professionals: orthodontists and general-practice dentists. Dental professionals' choice of a treatment method is determined by the following key considerations: the aesthetic appeal of the treatment method, the effectiveness of treatment,

This section identifies the key collaborators that will facilitate the success of the Invisalign system.

comfort associated with the treatment method, oral hygiene, ease of use, predictability of the treatment outcome, the level of customer support, dental professionals' chair time, and price.

We expect dental professionals to contribute to the success of the Invisalign system by (1) informing patients about the availability and benefits of the Invisalign system, (2) implementing the Invisalign treatment, and (3) providing performance feedback that will enable us to improve the Invisalign system. We expect general-practice dentists to treat primarily mild cases of malocclusion and refer more complex cases to licensed orthodontists.

We have trained 8,310 orthodontists and 27,480 general practice dentists in the United States and 12,340 dental professionals, predominantly orthodontists, internationally. The quarterly utilization rate of Invisalign among dental professionals is 4.9 cases per participating orthodontist, 2.3 cases per participating general-practice dentist, and 3.1 cases per non-US dental professional.

Competitors

Our competitors include the manufacturers of traditional orthodontic products that treat malocclusion, such as 3M Company, Sybron International Corporation, and Dentsply International, Inc. In addition, in the past years a number of direct competitors emerged, including *Clear Guide*, *Simpli5*, and *Red, White, and Blue System* by Allesee Orthodontic Appliances (AOA), a subsidiary of Sybron Dental Specialties, Inc.; *Incognito* braces by 3M; *Clearguide Express* by Insignia; MTM aligners by Dentsply International; *Damon Clear* and *Inspire ICE* by Ormco; *SureSmile* by Orametix; and *ClearCorrect*.

This section identifies the key competitors for the Invisalign system and evaluates the current and future competitive intensity of the marketplace.

Company

Align Technology Inc. was incorporated in Delaware in 1997. The corporate headquarters are located in Santa Clara, California, where we house our manufacturing, customer support, software engineering, and administrative personnel. In addition, we operate facilities in Mexico, Costa Rica, Europe, and Japan.

This section provides general information about the company and its current offerings.

We currently have 1,307 employees, including 641 in manufacturing and operations, 340 in sales and marketing, 154 in research and development, and 172 in general and administrative functions. Geographically, our employees are located as follows: 576 in the United States, 586 in Costa Rica, 134 in Europe, and 11 in Japan.

Our primary goal is to establish the Invisalign system as the standard method for treating orthodontic malocclusion. Our core competency is producing highly customized, close tolerance, medical-quality products in volume. Our strategic assets include intellectual property (proprietary patented technology), specialized production facilities, our network of dental professionals trained to use the Invisalign system, the Invisalign and ClinCheck brands, and our existing customer base.

Context

Economic context: Economic crisis, increasing stock market volatility, mortgage crisis, plummeting housing market, credit crunch threatening the solvency of the banking system, and declining consumer confidence and spending.

Regulatory context: Laws regulating medical device manufacturers and healthcare providers cover a broad array of subjects, including:

- The confidentiality of patient medical information and the circumstances under which such information may be released for inclusion in our databases, or released by us to third parties, are subject to substantial regulation by state governments.

- Federal and state regulations prohibit paying any remuneration in exchange for the referral of patients to a person participating in federal or state healthcare programs, such as Medicare and Medicaid.

- Various states regulate the operation of an advertising and referral service for dentists and may require compliance with various requirements on how they structure their relationships with participating dentists.

- According to the FDA classification of medical devices, the Invisalign system is a Class I device, the least stringent class, that does not require a premarket approval, which includes, among other things, extensive preclinical and clinical trials.

- Our global operations are subject to a variety of local regulations that define the relationships between Align Technology, dental professionals, and patients.

> This section outlines the specifics of the context in which Align Technology will fulfill the needs of its target customers.

4.2. Customer Value Proposition

Value Proposition

The Invisalign system offers a number of unique benefits to our target customers:

- *Excellent aesthetics.* Aligners are nearly invisible when worn, eliminating the aesthetic concerns associated with conventional braces.

- *Improved oral hygiene.* Patients can remove Aligners when eating, brushing, and flossing — a feature that can reduce tooth decay and periodontal damage during treatment.

- *Greater safety.* By replacing the six-week adjustment cycle of traditional braces with two-week stages, the Invisalign system moves teeth more gently, decreasing the likelihood of root resorption (shortening of tooth roots).

- *Increased comfort.* The Invisalign system is substantially more comfortable and less abrasive than conventional braces.

- *Reduced overall treatment time.* The Invisalign system controls force by distributing it broadly over the exposed surfaces of the

> Section 4.2 follows the 3-V framework

> This section outlines the key benefits of the Invisalign system for target customers. It answers the question: *Why would target customers opt to straighten their teeth using the Invisalign system?*

teeth while at the same time reducing the likelihood of unintended tooth movements. This could significantly reduce overall treatment time relative to conventional braces.

- *Reduced incidence of emergencies.* Lost or broken Aligners could be simply replaced with the next Aligner in the series, minimizing inconvenience to both patient and orthodontist.

Positioning Statement

For adults and teens with mild forms of malocclusion, Invisalign offers a convenient and unobtrusive solution to straighten their teeth.

This section identifies target customers and Invisalign's main benefit for these customers.

4.3. Collaborator Value Proposition

Value Proposition

The Invisalign system offers the following benefits to dental professionals:

- *Ability to visualize treatment and likely outcomes.* The Invisalign system enables dental professionals to preview a course of treatment and the likely final outcome of treatment in an interactive three-dimensional computer model. This allows dental professionals to analyze multiple treatment alternatives before selecting the one most appropriate for the patient.

- *Ease of use.* Because the Invisalign system relies on the same biomechanical principles that underlie traditional orthodontic treatment, it is straightforward for dental professionals to learn and to use. The initial certification training can be completed in a one-day workshop, and dental professionals can be equipped to submit cases immediately thereafter with minimal financial outlay.

- *Increased patient base.* Currently, only one percent of the more than 200 million people with malocclusion in the United States enter treatment each year. The Invisalign system allows dental professionals to broaden their patient base by offering a new, attractive treatment alternative to people who would not otherwise elect treatment.

- *Higher margins.* The Invisalign system enables dental professionals to more accurately estimate the duration of the treatment, thus decreasing the likelihood of underestimating the treatment length and increasing the overall profit margins per patient. Due to the substantial benefits for customers, orthodontists can also charge a premium for the Invisalign system comparable to other more aesthetically pleasing alternatives to conventional braces, such as ceramic and lingual braces.

- *Decreased orthodontist and staff time.* The Invisalign system reduces both the frequency and length of patient visits. It eliminates the need for time-intensive processes, such as bonding appliances to the patient's teeth, adjusting archwires during the course of treatment, and removing the appliances at the

This section outlines the key benefits of the Invisalign system for dental professionals. It answers the question: Why would dental professionals opt to use the Invisalign system instead of conventional braces?

conclusion of treatment. As a result, use of the Invisalign system significantly reduces orthodontist and staff chair time and can increase practice throughput.

Positioning Statement

For dental professionals, the Invisalign system is the best method for treating most cases of malocclusion because it offers increased patient volume and higher margins.

4.4. Company Value Proposition

This section identifies the company's collaborators and the key benefit of the offering for these collaborators.

Value Proposition

In 2007, our total revenues were $271 million; our gross margin was 73.6% and our operating margin was 12.5%. In 2008, we intend to improve our financial performance by increasing our revenues by 10%, our gross margin to 75%, and our operating margin to 14%. Detailed financial information and the key assumptions are provided in Exhibits 1-2.

This section outlines the key benefits for shareholders. It answers the question: Why should stakeholders invest in Invisalign?

Positioning Statement

For investors who are interested in investing in a company with a high growth potential, Align Technology offers an opportunity to participate in a $75 billion market for orthodontic devices with a patented system that offers unique benefits for both patients and dental professionals.

This section identifies the key stakeholders and the key benefit of the Invisalign system for them.

5. Tactics

5.1. Product

The Invisalign system consists of two components: ClinCheck and Aligners.

- *ClinCheck* is an interactive Internet application that allows dental professionals to diagnose and plan treatment for their patients. ClinCheck uses a dental impression and a treatment prescription submitted by the dental professional to develop a customized, three-dimensional treatment plan that simulates appropriate tooth movement in a series of two-week increments. ClinCheck allows dental professionals to view this three-dimensional simulation with a high degree of magnification and from any angle.

- *Aligners* are custom-manufactured, clear, removable dental appliances that, when worn in the prescribed series provide orthodontic treatment. Each Aligner covers a patient's teeth and is nearly invisible when worn. Aligners are commonly worn in pairs (over the upper and lower dental arches) for consecutive two-week periods that correspond to the approved ClinCheck treatment simulation. After two weeks of use, the patient discards the Aligners and replaces them with the next pair in the series. This process is repeated until the final Aligners are used and treatment is complete.

Section 5.1 outlines the product aspect of the Invisalign system and the proposed product changes.

The ClinCheck application can also be viewed as part of the service aspect of the Invisalign system (dental professionals do not acquire the rights to the software application but merely gain the right to use it on a limited basis); however, because it is an essential element of creating the product (Aligners), it is presented as a component of the product aspect of the offering.

At present, we offer two treatment programs: Invisalign Full and Invisalign Express (introduced in 2005).

- *Invisalign Full* treatment consists of as many Aligners as indicated by ClinCheck in order to achieve treatment goals. The typical Invisalign Full patient uses 22 sets of Aligners over 44 weeks of treatment.

- *Invisalign Express* is intended to assist dental professionals in treating a broader range of patients by providing a lower cost option for adult relapse cases, minor crowding and spacing, or as a precursor to restorative or cosmetic treatment, such as veneers. Invisalign Express consists of up to 10 Aligners.

In 2008, we plan to launch two new treatment programs: Invisalign Teen and Vivera retainers.

- *Invisalign Teen* is designed to treat teenagers (age 12 and up) whose teeth are still growing. It includes features such as an Aligner-wear indicator to help gauge patient compliance and specially engineered Aligner features to address lingual root control issues and the natural eruption of key teeth common in teen patients. Invisalign Teen will also include up to six free individual replacement Aligners during active treatment to cover potential Aligner loss. We plan to introduce Invisalign Teen in the second quarter of 2008.

- *Vivera* is a retainer replacement program that delivers a new retainer to orthodontic patients every three months for one year. Vivera retainers are produced using the same proprietary technology and material as the Invisalign Aligners, and offer an effective, aesthetic retention solution for both Invisalign and non-Invisalign patients. We plan to introduce Vivera retainers in the first quarter of 2008.

A detailed description of product specifications is offered in Exhibit 3.

5.2. Service

We offer support services to orthodontists who elect to use the Invisalign system. These services include initial training, case support, and practice-building assistance.

- *Initial training* is conducted in a workshop format by our sales and orthodontic teams. The key topics covered in training include case selection criteria, instructions on filling out the Invisalign prescription form, guidance on pricing, and instructions on interacting with the ClinCheck software and using the Invisalign website.

- *Current-case support* includes assisting orthodontists with the applicability and use of the Invisalign system for specific patients.

- *Practice-building assistance* helps orthodontists promote their services to local general-practice dentists and to prospective patients through direct mail or other media.

Section 5.2 outlines the service aspect of the Invisalign system, focusing on the service provided to dental professionals using the Invisalign system. This section also outlines the proposed changes in the service provided to dental professionals.

In 2008, we plan to introduce two new services: *Invisalign Assist* and *Aligntech Institute*.

- *Invisalign Assist* is designed specifically for general-practice dentists who prefer an integrated approach to selecting, monitoring, and finishing Invisalign cases. Intended to help newly trained and low-volume general-practice dentists accelerate the adoption and frequency of use of Invisalign in their practice, Invisalign Assist is intended to make it easier for general-practice dentists to select appropriate cases for their experience level or treatment approach, submit cases more efficiently, and manage appointments with suggested tasks. New progress tracking features allow dentists to submit new impressions every nine stages and receive Aligners modified according to the patients' progress.

- The *Aligntech Institute* program consolidates our extensive clinical education programs within a new interactive website (www.aligntechinstitute.com) that will provide clinical education and practice development training opportunities for our Invisalign-trained dental professionals on demand. These practice-development training opportunities will include instructor-led training classes, seminars and workshops, conference calls, online videos, case studies, and other clinical resources.

A detailed description of Invisalign Assist and Aligntech Institute is offered in Exhibit 4.

5.3. Brand

We use two brands to identify our offering: Invisalign and ClinCheck.

- *Invisalign.* We use the brand Invisalign in reference to the process of straightening teeth using a series of invisible Aligners. We use the Invisalign brand in our communication to consumers, orthodontists, and general-practice dentists. The Invisalign name is our registered trademark. The Invisalign brand is also used as an umbrella brand for two sub-brands: Invisalign Full and Invisalign Express.

- *ClinCheck.* We use the brand ClinCheck in reference to the interactive Internet application that allows dental professionals to diagnose and plan treatment for their patients. We use the ClinCheck brand in our communication to dental professionals; it is not used in consumer communication. The ClinCheck name is our registered trademark.

In 2008, we plan to reposition the Invisalign brand and extend our brand portfolio.

- *Repositioning the Invisalign brand.* We plan to reposition our brand to strengthen our brand recognition and better align it with our strategic initiatives. The new look and feel of Invisalign is dynamic, modern, and approachable, and communicates our vision of "healthy, beautiful smiles" in a way

Section 5.3 outlines the brands used by Align Technology to create a unique identity for its offering.

Note that while both brands—ClinCheck and Invisalign—are promoted to dental professionals, only the latter is used in consumer communication.

This section also outlines the proposed changes to the Invisalign brand.

that is distinct and memorable. Our brand repositioning strategy is based on the findings of our proprietary research and aims to increase Invisalign awareness and demand among consumers, and Invisalign adoption and utilization by dental professionals.

- *Extending our brand portfolio.* We plan to add two new Invisalign sub-brands: *Invisalign Teen* and *Invisalign Assist.* We will also introduce two new brands: *Vivera,* used with retainers, and the *Aligntech Institute* brand, which consolidates our educational programs. We have filed applications for these trademarks with the US Patent and Trademarks Office.

A detailed description of the Invisalign, Aligntech, and Vivera logos is offered in Exhibit 5.

5.4. Pricing

The price for the orthodontic treatment is negotiated by the dental professional and the patient. The average retail price for the orthodontists' services (including Aligners) is around $5,000 to $7,000 depending on the severity of the case.

Align Technology's products are offered to dental professionals on a fixed-price (rather than per-Aligner) basis. The average price for dental professionals is $1,500 per patient for Invisalign Full; $1,000 for Invisalign Express; $1,700 for Invisalign Teen; $1,900 for Invisalign Assist, and $200 for Vivera retainers. Detailed pricing information is shown in Exhibit 6.

5.5. Incentives

We offer incentives to both our target customers and collaborators.

- *Incentives for customers.* Because the specifics and the cost of the treatment are negotiated directly between the dental professional and the patient, we are not offering direct incentives to consumers. We expect dental professionals to offer their own discounts to customers to manage demand.

- *Incentives for collaborators.* We use a system of tiering dental professionals that encourages our sales force to devote more time to those dental professionals most proficient in the use of the Invisalign system. We use objective criteria, primarily the number of cases initiated with the Invisalign system, to tier dental professionals. Inquiries from prospective patients through our customer call center and our website are directed to higher tier dental professionals. This tiering process should incentivize the selected dental professionals and increase the use of the Invisalign system by their offices. A detailed description of collaborator incentives is offered in Exhibit 7.

Section 5.4 outlines the price of the Invisalign system for both patients and dental professionals.

Note that the Invisalign system is only one component of the treatment and that the dental professionals determine the customer price.

Section 5.5 outlines the incentives provided to target customers and collaborators.

5.6. Communication

Consumer Communication

Consumers can learn about the benefits of the Invisalign system in one of two ways: directly from us and/or from dental professionals. Accordingly, we use two basic strategies to reach our target customers. We use a *pull strategy* (direct-to-consumer communication) to target appearance-conscious consumers who might not consider orthodontic treatment unless they are made aware of the existence of an aesthetically appealing malocclusion treatment. In addition, we use a *push strategy* (incentivizing dental professionals) to target health-conscious individuals who rely on dental professionals' advice for the choice of treatment.

- *Direct-to-consumer (pull) communication.*

  Media. We promote the Invisalign system by communicating its benefits directly to consumers with a nationwide television and radio advertising campaign. We also provide consumers with information through our toll-free phone line (1-800-INVISIBLE) and our website (invisalign.com).

  Message. Because the direct-to-consumer campaign targets appearance-conscious consumers, our message will focus on the aesthetic benefits and the overall convenience of using the Invisalign system.

  Slogan. Our slogan is "Learn how to smile again."

- *Indirect (push) consumer communication.* To facilitate recommendations of the Invisalign system, we provide orthodontists and general-practice dentists with promotional materials—brochures, calendars, and posters to be displayed in their offices and/or given to patients who express interest.

Our consumer communication is outlined in Exhibit 8.

Collaborator Communication

Dental professionals can learn about the Invisalign system from our mass-media consumer advertising as well as from our communication that targets dental professionals.

- *Media.* We use print advertisements in the professional press targeting dental professionals, event sponsorship for orthodontic and dental conventions and conferences, as well as direct mail and telemarketing targeting individual orthodontic and dental practices. In addition, we have a sales team comprising 136 direct sales representatives in North America and over 30 people engaged in sales and sales support internationally.

- *Message.* Our message focuses on the potential to substantially improve dental practice profitability through increased patient volume and higher margins.

Additional information on our communication to dental professionals is provided in Exhibit 9.

This section outlines the communication to target customers and the proposed changes in this communication.

Note that the use of a pull vs. push strategy in the case of direct vs. indirect communication follows directly from the analysis of the target market in Section 4.1.

The content of the message to target customers follows directly from the value proposition and the positioning statement outlined in Section 4.2.

This section outlines the communication to dental professionals and the proposed changes in this communication.

The content of the message to dental professionals follows directly from the value proposition and the positioning statement outlined in Section 4.3.

5.7. Distribution

The Invisalign system is distributed exclusively through orthodontists and general-practice dentists; it is not available for retail purchase by consumers directly from Align Technology. Orders are processed through headquarters and shipped in batches directly to dental offices from the manufacturing facilities in Mexico as follows:

- *Invisalign Full* and *Invisalign Express* aligners are delivered to orthodontists and general-practice dentists in a single shipment.

- *Invisalign Teen* aligners (other than the replacement aligners) will be available only to orthodontists and will be delivered in a single shipment.

- *Invisalign Assist* aligners will be shipped to dentists using progress tracking after every nine stages.

- *Vivera* retainers will be shipped to orthodontists and general-practice dentists every three months over a one-year period.

Section 5.7 outlines the distribution channel for the Invisalign system and the proposed changes in the distribution system.

6. Implementation

Section 6 outlines the processes involved in implementing the marketing plan.

6.1. Resource Development

At present, we have the essential resources to implement our business plan. We are continuing the development of automated systems for the fabrication and packaging of Aligners manufactured in Mexico. We also plan to increase the efficiency of our manufacturing processes by focusing our efforts on software development and improving the efficiency of operations in Costa Rica. A detailed outline of the proposed changes is provided in Exhibit 10.

6.2. Developing the Market Offering

We are currently engaged in the design, manufacture, promotion, and distribution of Invisalign Full and Invisalign Express. A detailed description of the implementation processes in managing Align Technology offerings is provided in Exhibit 11.

6.3. Commercial Deployment

We plan to launch Vivera retainers in the first quarter of 2008, Invisalign Teen in the second quarter of 2008, and Invisalign Assist in the third quarter of 2008. The detailed schedule for the commercial deployment of these offerings is outlined in Exhibit 12.

7. Control

7.1. Performance Evaluation

We are constantly monitoring our financial performance to ensure that we are on track toward achieving our goals. In addition to the standard financial metrics reported in our financial statements, we use the following metrics to monitor our performance:

Section 7.1 outlines the metrics used to measure the progress toward the goal defined in Section 3.

- Number of patients initiating treatment using our products
- Number of dental professionals trained to use the Invisalign system
- Penetration rate (number of dental professionals who have used the Invisalign system during the past 12 months)
- Utilization rate (number of cases ordered per dental professional during each quarter)

We actively solicit feedback from orthodontists and general-practice dentists to improve the technology underlying the Invisalign system.

7.2. Analysis of the Environment

We constantly monitor for changes in the environment, including:

- Changes in customer preferences
- Changes in our internal resources and competencies
- Changes in the value the Invisalign system delivers to our collaborators (orthodontists and general-practice dentists)
- Changes in the competitive landscape
- Changes in the economic, business, sociocultural, technological, and regulatory context in which the company operates

To monitor the environment, we engage in the following activities:

- Monitor the USPTO database for new patent and trademark applications
- Participate in professional conferences and trade shows
- Examine professional publications
- Conduct proprietary research to examine consumer and dental professionals' experience with our offerings
- Review secondary research dealing with new developments in orthodontic technology and marketing practices

Performance metrics are outlined in detail in Exhibit 13.

8. Exhibits

Exhibit 1 – Exhibit 13.

Section 7.2 outlines the process of monitoring for changes in the environment in which the company operates.

Section 8 outlines documentation supporting the marketing plan (for brevity, the actual exhibits are not included in this plan).

CHAPTER SIX

SAMPLE MARKETING PLAN: DEWALT INDUSTRIAL TOOL COMPANY

The sample marketing plan outlined in this section depicts Black & Decker's launch of DeWalt Industrial Tool Company. At the time of launch, Black & Decker was the world's larger manufacturer of power tools, electric lawn and garden tools, and residential security hardware. Despite its success in consumer and industrial markets, Black & Decker was underperforming in the tradesman segment — consisting of small businesses and independent contractors. Recognizing the growth potential of this segment and its strategic importance in gaining market position, Black & Decker made the decision to launch a new product line designed specifically to address the needs of tradesmen. The new product line would be managed by a separate company, organized as a wholly owned subsidiary of Black & Decker and carrying the name of one of the brands in Black &Decker's portfolio — DeWalt.

DeWalt's marketing plan illustrates the launch of a new brand under the auspices of the newly created strategic business unit (DeWalt Industrial Tool Company) of Black & Decker. The launch of the new offering is positioned in the context of an existing product line targeting three different customer segments: consumer, industrial, and tradesman. In this context, the marketing plan illustrates DeWalt's strategy for optimizing the value for its customers, collaborators, and the company. DeWalt's marketing plan further highlights the specifics of the different elements of the marketing mix — product, service, brand, price, incentives, communication, and distribution — that carry out the proposed strategy.[5]

The DeWalt marketing plan outlined in this chapter follows the structure of the plan outlined earlier in this book. It comprises an *executive summary* that outlines the highlights of the marketing plan, a *situation overview* that offers background information on the market in which the company operates, an *action plan* that follows the G-STIC framework, and a set of *exhibits* that provides additional information about specific aspects of the marketing plan. To better illustrate the relationship among the different elements of the marketing plan, the purpose of each section and the links between different sections of the marketing plan are highlighted in the sidebar.

MARKETING PLAN
DeWalt Industrial Tool Company[6]

1. Executive Summary

Black & Decker's power tools division represents the largest product group, accounting for 29% of the company's US revenue.

The power tools market comprises three segments: consumer, industrial, and tradesman. Although Black & Decker is the market leader in the consumer and industrial segments, it has only 9% share of the tradesman segment. Furthermore, despite the strength of Black & Decker's brand and the quality of its tools, the company profitability in this segment was virtually zero.

This plan outlines our key marketing activities directed at establishing Black & Decker's market leadership in the tradesman segment by launching a new set of products and services under the DeWalt brand.

The executive summary in Section 1 offers a succinct overview of the key aspects of the offering.

2. Situation Overview

The power tools market comprises three types of customers: (1) *consumers*—buyers who use power tools around the house, (2) *tradesmen*—small businesses and independent contractors, such as carpenters, plumbers, and electricians working in residential construction—using power tools on the job; and (3) *industrial buyers*, such as companies that purchase power tools for employee use.

The key attributes that customers typically consider when making a choice are: power, reliability, service, brand image, and price. The relative importance of these factors for each of the three segments is shown below:

Section 2 identifies an unmet customer need that the company aims to fulfill with its offering.

Key Customer Segments in the Power Tool Market

	Customer segments		
Attributes	Consumer	Tradesman	Industrial
Power	Low	High	High
Reliability	Low	High	High
Service	Low	High	Medium
Brand	Medium	High	Low
Price	High	Low	Medium

Power tools are distributed through a variety of channels that include industrial supply companies (W. W. Grainger), wholesale distributors (serving smaller retailers), large home improvement centers (Home Depot, Lowe's), smaller hardware chains (Ace Hardware, ServiStar), independently owned hardware stores, and mass-merchandisers (Walmart, Kmart).

The key competitors in the US power tool market include Black & Decker, Makita, Milwaukee Tools, Ryobi, Skill, Craftsman (manufactured by Black & Decker and sold as a private label by Sears), Porter-Cable, Bosch, Hitachi, Panasonic, and Hilti.

Black & Decker is the world's larger manufacturer of power tools, electric lawn and garden tools, and residential security hardware. Black & Decker's five largest product groups are: power tools (29% of Black & Decker's US sales), household products (15%), information systems and services (11%), outdoor products (9%), and security hardware (9%). Black & Decker is the market share leader in the power tools segment, which is the largest contributor to Black & Decker's growth. The Black & Decker brand was frequently ranked among the top ten most powerful brands in the United States.

Black & Decker targets all three customer segments: consumer, tradesman, and industrial. Due to Black & Decker's subpar performance in the tradesmen segment, the focus of this plan is on the tradesmen.

3. Goal

Our *primary goal* is to improve the share of Black & Decker in the power tool market from 9% to 20% in three years.

To achieve our primary goal, we have set the following objectives:

- *Customer objectives.* Gain awareness, build preference, and foster adoption of the DeWalt brand by tradesmen.

- *Collaborator objectives.* Ensure product availability and promotional support by the distribution channels catering to the tradesman segment.

- *Internal objectives.* Improve operating income from 10% to 12%.

- *Competitive objectives.* Focus marketing efforts on stealing share from Makita, identified as the key competitor in the tradesman segment.

Section 3 outlines the company's primary goal, as well as a series of sub-goals (objectives) focusing on customers, collaborators, the company, and competitors.

4. Strategy

4.1. Target Market

Customers

Our target customers are tradesmen—small businesses and independent contractors working in residential construction and using power tools on the job.

- *Value potential*: Tradesmen represent 28% ($420M) of the US power tools market and are the fastest growing (9%) segment of this market.

- *Value drivers*: Performance (power, precision, and ergonomics), reliability, service, and brand image.

Section 4.1 follows the 5-C framework.

This section identifies the offering's target customers.

- *Demographic profile:* Small businesses and independent contractors (carpenters, plumbers, and electricians) working in residential construction.

- *Behavioral profile:* Use power tools on the job; read trade press (*Builder* and *Electrical Contractor*); and visit trade shows and home improvement stores, including large home improvement centers, such as Home Depot and Lowe's, and smaller hardware chains, such as Ace Hardware and ServiStar; and independently owned hardware stores.

A detailed description of DeWalt's customers is given in Exhibit 1.

Company

DeWalt Industrial Tool Company is a strategic business unit of Black & Decker. A detailed description of DeWalt is given in Exhibit 2.

Collaborators

Distribution channel partners: Wholesale distributors (serving smaller retailers), large home improvement centers (Home Depot, Lowe's), smaller hardware chains (Ace Hardware, ServiStar), and independently owned hardware stores. A detailed description of DeWalt's collaborators is given in Exhibit 3.

This section identifies the key collaborators that will facilitate the success of DeWalt offerings.

Competitors

Makita Electric (50% market share), Milwaukee Tools (10% market share), Ryobi (9% market share), Skill (5%), Craftsman (5%), Porter-Cable (3%), and Bosch (3%). A detailed description of DeWalt's competitors is given in Exhibit 4.

This section identifies the key competitors.

Context

- *Economic context:* Recession, resulting in high unemployment, limited money supply (credit), increased inflation, rapid growth of new home construction and remodeling prior to the recession, and rise of big box home improvement centers such as The Home Depot and Lowe's.

- *Regulatory context:* Price dumping allegations against some of the Japanese manufacturers, including Makita, raising the possibility of imposing import duties on certain tools imported from Japan.

Section 4.1.5 outlines the specifics of the context in which Black & Decker will launch the DeWalt product line.

4.2. Customer Value Proposition

Section 4.2 follows the 3-V framework

Value Proposition

Our value proposition for tradesmen is offering high-performance, reliable tools backed by a national service and quality commitment unparalleled in the power tool industry. Our offerings will deliver greater value to tradesmen than the competition on each of the key attributes important to tradesmen as shown in the following table (the first set of ratings reflect the importance of each attribute to tradesmen and the remaining ratings reflect the performance of each competitor on these attributes):

This section outlines the key benefits of DeWalt products for target customers. It identifies the key drivers of customer value and highlights DeWalt's competitive advantage.

DeWalt Value Proposition for Tradesmen

Attributes	Attribute importance	Market offerings			
		DeWalt	Makita	Milwaukee	Ryobi
Power	High	High	High	High	Medium
Reliability	High	High	High	High	High
Service	High	High	Medium	Medium	Low
Brand	High	High	High	High	Low
Price	Low	High	High	High	Medium

Positioning Statement

For the tradesman who uses power tools to make a living, DeWalt offers dependable professional tools that are engineered to be tough and are backed by a guarantee of repair or replacement within 48 hours.

> This section identifies target customers and the main benefits of the DeWalt offering for these customers.

4.3. Collaborator Value Proposition

Value Proposition

- *Monetary value:* Potential to increase sales volume and profit margins.
- *Strategic value:* Increased customer traffic supported by a large promotional budget, streamlining the procurement process by having a single supplier for both consumer and professional segments, and price protection from discount retailers.

> This section outlines the key benefits of the DeWalt offering for collaborators.

Positioning Statement

DeWalt power tools are a better choice for retailers than Makita because they offer price protection from discount retailers.

> This section outlines DeWalt's positioning statement.

4.4. Company Value Proposition

Value Proposition

- *Monetary value:* Potential to increase market share from 8% to 50% and increase margins from 5% to 10%. Increase the valuation of the company by creating a new brand.
- *Strategic value:* Ensures leadership positioning in the growing tradesman segment. Solidifies Black & Decker's relationship with retailers by offering an attractive product portfolio that enables retailers to have a single-source supplier for both consumer and professional segments.

> This section outlines the value of the offering for the company. Because the key aspects of company value are reflected in the company's goal, this section restates the goal outlined in Section 3.

Positioning Statement

DeWalt power tools are a great choice because they enable Black & Decker to achieve its profit goals.

> This section identifies the internal positioning of the DeWalt offering.

5. Tactics

5.1. Product

Thirty-three high-performing power tools (drills, saws, sanders, and plate joiners) and 323 accessories designed to maximize power, precision, ergonomics, and reliability, and designated to replace the Black & Decker Professional product line. DeWalt's product line is outlined in Exhibit 5.

Section 5.1 outlines the product aspect of the DeWalt offering.

5.2. Service

- *Loaner tool policy*: DeWalt will lend a tool for the repair period.
- *48-hour service policy:* If a repair is not completed within 48 hours, DeWalt will provide a new tool free of charge.
- *Technical support*: Experts are available by phone at 1-800-4DeWALT to offer assistance regarding DeWalt products, service, repair, or replacement.
- *Free one-year service contract*: DeWalt will maintain the tool and replace worn parts free during the first year of ownership.
- *One-year warranty:* DeWalt will warranty materials and workmanship for one year.
- *Superior diagnostics*. DeWalt Service Centers use state-of-the-art testing equipment to quickly diagnose problems.
- *Trade support*: Black & Decker will provide support for its channel partners to facilitate ordering, inventory management, and returns.

DeWalt's portfolio of services is outlined in Exhibit 6.

Section 5.2 outlines the service aspect of the DeWalt offering.

5.3. Brand

Brand Identifiers

- *Brand name*: DeWalt® (replaces the Black & Decker Professional brand)
- *Brand logo:* **DeWALT**.
- *Brand color:* Yellow

Brand Referents

- High-performance industrial tools
- Guaranteed tough
- "No downtime" company

Section 5.3 outlines the specifics of the DeWalt brand.

5.4. Price

Customer Pricing

- *Price:* Premium price tier (10% higher than Makita)
- *Returns:* DeWalt will accept returns for any reason within 30 days from the date of purchase

Section 5.4 outlines the price of DeWalt products for customers and distributors.

Distribution Channel Pricing

- *Price:* Trade margins 5% higher than Makita
- *Price protection:* Price protection from discounters (e.g., halting supplies to price-cutting retailers)

5.5. Incentives

Loyalty programs: Preferred contractor program (Exhibit 7)

Trade incentives: Trade incentives to ensure retailer support (Exhibit 8)

> Section 5.5 outlines customer and collaborator incentives.

5.6. Communication

Customer Communication

- *Message:* Create awareness of the new product line and service program; build the DeWalt brand to create customer loyalty. Taglines: *DeWalt. Guaranteed Tough* and *High Performance Industrial Tools*
- *Media:* Industry magazines (*Builder* and *Electrical Contractor*, $1M budget); trade shows, direct-mail catalogs ($300K budget); point-of-sale displays at home-improvement retailers, ten vans visiting job sites promoting DeWalt products ($1M budget)

A detailed description of DeWalt's communication is given in Exhibit 9.

> This section outlines the communication aimed at target customers.

Collaborator Communication

- *Message:* Create awareness of the new product line and service program; build the DeWalt brand to create retailer loyalty. Tagline: *There's only one thing about DeWalt that's not tough: Making a profit*
- *Media:* Trade shows (National Association of Home Builders trade show); Black & Decker sales force

> This section outlines the communication aimed at the company's collaborators.

5.7. Distribution

- *DeWalt products* are distributed through the existing Black & Decker channels offering direct distribution to large home-improvement centers (Home Depot/Lowe's) and indirect (wholesaler) distribution to smaller hardware chains (Ace Hardware/ServiStar) and independent hardware stores. There will be a $20M inventory buildup at launch to ensure product availability and avoid stock-outs.
- *DeWalt service* is offered through 117 Black & Decker authorized service centers with a dedicated DeWalt counter (Exhibit 10).

> Section 5.7 outlines the distribution channels for the DeWalt offering.

6. Implementation

6.1. Resource Development

DeWalt Industrial Tool Company utilizes the resources of Black & Decker for product development, manufacturing, service, promotion, distribution, and trade support. In addition, DeWalt is developing its own promotion and customer service team, designed to work exclusively with tradesmen. An overview of the key resources and the organizational structure of DeWalt Industrial Tool Company is outlined in Exhibit 11.

6.2. Developing the DeWalt Offering

The processes involved in designing, promoting, and distributing DeWalt products and services are outlined in detail in Exhibit 12.

6.3. Commercial Deployment

DeWalt offerings will be deployed nationwide along with a communication campaign targeting tradesmen. At the time of launch, all distribution outlets outlined in section 5.7 will carry a large inventory of DeWalt products to ensure sufficient availability. In addition, all Black & Decker service centers will be ready to support DeWalt products. The specifics of the commercial deployment of the offering are outlined in Exhibit 13.

7. Control

7.1. Performance Evaluation

The key performance metrics include market share, operating income, customer satisfaction, and retail availability. We evaluate DeWalt's performance on these metrics on a quarterly basis and provide a comprehensive analysis at the end of the fiscal year. The specifics of our performance evaluation metrics are given in Exhibit 14.

7.2. Analysis of the Environment

We monitor the environment for changes in the needs of our customers and collaborators, changes in the competitive environment, and changes in the economic, technological, sociocultural, regulatory, and physical context in which we operate. In the absence of a major change in the environment, we evaluate these factors on a quarterly basis and provide a comprehensive analysis at the end of the fiscal year.

8. Exhibits

Exhibit 1 – Exhibit 14.

Section 6. outlines the processes involved in implementing the marketing plan.

Section 7.1 outlines the key metrics used to measure the progress toward the goal defined in Section 3.

Section 7.2 outlines the process of monitoring for changes in the environment in which the company operates.

Section 8 outlines documentation supporting the marketing plan (for brevity, the actual exhibits are not included).

PART THREE

MARKETING PLAN TOOLBOX

Introduction

This section presents a set of practical tools designed to facilitate the processes of strategic planning and developing a marketing plan. To this end, this section includes seven appendices that highlight different aspects of developing and writing actionable marketing plans that produce results.

- **Appendix A** presents a *template* for developing actionable marketing plans that can enable a company to achieve its strategic goals.

- **Appendix B** lays out the key principles of writing a *positioning statement* for a company's offering.

- **Appendix C** outlines the key principles of developing a *communication plan* as a component of the overarching marketing plan.

- **Appendix D** presents the key principles of developing meaningful *exhibits* to supplement the marketing plan.

- **Appendix E** outlines the *performance metrics and analyses* commonly used in developing a marketing plan. These metrics are grouped into three categories: company metrics, which reflect a company's progress toward achieving its strategic goal(s); customer metrics, which capture customers' response to the company's actions; and marketing mix metrics, which depict an offering's performance on different attributes: product, service, brand, price, incentives, communication, and distribution.

- **Appendix F** outlines several additional *frameworks* — the SWOT framework, the five forces framework, the product–market growth framework, the 4-P framework, the product life cycle framework, the critical path method, the responsibility assignment matrix, and the Gantt matrix — that are commonly used in marketing planning and analysis.

- **Appendix D** offers definitions of some of the *essential marketing concepts* commonly used in marketing planning and analysis.

Marketing Plan Template

Everything should be made as simple as possible, but not simpler.
— Albert Einstein, theoretical physicist

The development of a marketing plan is facilitated by following a standardized outline that delineates the key components of the plan and defines their contents. The marketing plan template outlined below follows the structure delineated in Chapter 3 and exemplified in Chapters 4–6.

Because the plans for launching a new offering and developing an existing one share a similar structure, the template shown here applies to both scenarios. The main text reflects an outline of a marketing plan for launching a new offering, and the text in square brackets indicates the additional information that needs to be included when developing a plan for managing an existing offering.

================================
Marketing Plan
Company | Offering
Planning period
================================

1. Executive Summary
Provide a brief overview of the situation, the company's goal, and the proposed course of action.

2. Situation Overview
Provide an overview of the situation (current/potential customers, collaborators, competitors, and context) in which the company operates and identify relevant opportunities and threats. [Provide an overview of the company's progress toward its current goals. Highlight the recent changes in the market (e.g., changes in buyer preferences, a new competitive entry, and a change in the regulatory environment).]

3. Goal
Identify the company's primary goal and market-specific objectives.

3.1. Primary Goal

Identify the company's ultimate goal by defining its focus (e.g., net income) and key performance benchmarks (e.g., quantify the desired net income and set the time frame for achieving it). [State the company's current progress toward this goal.]

3.2. Market Objectives

Identify the relevant customer, collaborator, company, competitive, and context objectives that will facilitate achieving the primary goal. Define the focus and key performance benchmarks for each objective. [State the company's current progress toward each objective.]

4. Strategy

Identify the target market and define the offering's value proposition. [Underscore the key changes to the current strategy.]

4.1. Target Market

Identify the target market—customers, collaborators, the company, competitors, and context—in which the company will launch its new offering. [Underscore the key changes in the target market.]

Customers

Define the need(s) to be fulfilled by the offering and identify the profile of customers with such needs. [Identify any recent changes in customer needs/profile.]

Collaborators

Identify the key collaborators (e.g., suppliers, channel members, and communication partners) and their strategic goals. [Identify any recent changes in collaborators.]

Company

Define the strategic business unit responsible for the offering, the relevant personnel, and key stakeholders. Outline the company's core competencies and strategic assets, its current product line, and market position. [Identify any recent changes in the company's core competencies and strategic assets, its current product line, and market position.]

Competitors

Identify the competitive offerings that provide similar benefits to target customers and collaborators. [Underscore any recent changes in the competitive environment.]

Context

Evaluate the relevant economic, technological, sociocultural, regulatory, and physical context. [Identify any recent changes in the relevant context.]

4.2. Value Proposition

Define the offering's value proposition for target customers, collaborators, and the company.

Customer Value Proposition

Define the offering's value proposition, positioning strategy, and positioning statement for target customers. [Highlight the proposed changes in the customer value proposition.]

Collaborator Value Proposition

Define the offering's value proposition, positioning strategy, and positioning statement for collaborators. [Highlight the proposed changes in the collaborator value proposition.]

Company Value Proposition

Outline the offering's value proposition, positioning strategy, and positioning statement for company stakeholders and personnel. [Highlight the proposed changes in the company value proposition.]

5. Tactics

Outline the key attributes of the market offering: product, service, brand, price, incentives, communication, and distribution. [Highlight the proposed changes in tactics.]

5.1. Product

Define relevant product characteristics (attributes, benefits, and costs). [Highlight the proposed product changes.]

5.2. Service

Identify relevant service characteristics (attributes, benefits, and costs). [Highlight the proposed service changes.]

5.3. Brand

Determine the key elements defining the identity and the meaning of the brand. [Highlight the proposed changes to the brand.]

5.4. Price

Identify the price(s) at which the offering is provided to customers and channel members. [Highlight the proposed price changes.]

5.5. Incentives

Define the incentives offered to customers (e.g., price reductions), collaborators (e.g., trade allowances), and company personnel (e.g., bonuses). [Highlight the proposed changes to incentives.]

5.6. Communication

Identify the manner in which the key aspects of the offering (product, service, brand, price, and incentives) are communicated to target customers, collaborators, and company employees and stakeholders. [Highlight the proposed changes to communication.]

5.7. Distribution

Describe the manner in which the offering is delivered to target customers, collaborators, and the company. [Highlight the proposed changes to the distribution.]

6. Implementation

Define the specifics of implementing the company's offering. [Highlight the proposed implementation changes.]

6.1. Resource Development

Identify the key resources needed to implement the marketing plan and outline a process for developing/acquiring deficient resources. [Highlight the proposed changes in the current resource-development approach.]

6.2. Offering Development

Outline the processes for developing the market offering. [Highlight the proposed changes to the current process of developing the offering.]

6.3. Commercial Deployment

Delineate the process for bringing the offering to target customers. [Highlight the proposed changes in the current market-deployment approach.]

7. Control

Identify the metrics used to measure the company's performance and monitor the environment in which the company operates. [Highlight the proposed changes in the controls.]

7.1. Performance Evaluation

Define the criteria for evaluating the company's performance and progress toward the set goals. [Highlight the proposed changes in the metrics used to evaluate performance.]

7.2. Analysis of the Environment

Identify metrics for evaluating the environment in which the company operates and outline the processes for modifying the plan to accommodate changes in the environment. [Highlight the proposed changes in the metrics used to evaluate the environment and modify the action plan.]

8. Exhibits

Provide additional information to support specific aspects of the marketing plan. This information may include target market data (e.g., industry overview, company overview, and customer trend analyses); financial calculations (e.g., break-even analysis, best/worst case scenario analysis, and customer value analysis); details pertaining to the marketing mix (e.g., product specifications, communication plan, and distribution structure); implementation (e.g., an overview of the processes of developing and deploying the offering); and control (e.g., performance metrics and analysis of the environment).

Writing a Positioning Statement

I have only made this letter longer because
I have not had the time to make it shorter.
— Blaise Pascal, French mathematician and philosopher

The positioning statement is an internal company document that succinctly outlines an offering's strategy to guide tactical decisions. The positioning statement is a communication device that aims to share the offering's strategy with the relevant stakeholders involved in the development and management of a particular offering. The key principles of developing a positioning statement are the focus of this chapter.

Positioning Statement as a Means of Communication

The positioning statement is a succinct document — usually consisting of a single sentence — that delineates the key components of an offering's strategy. The primary purpose of the positioning statement is to guide tactical decisions related to the product, service, brand, price, incentives, communication, and distribution aspects of the offering. As such, the positioning statement seeks to communicate the essence of the offering's strategy to all stakeholders in order to ensure that their activities are aligned with the company's goals.

The positioning statement plays an important role because different managers within the company might not have an accurate understanding of the offering's strategy: who the offering's target customers are, why they would choose this offering over a competitor's, and how this offering benefits the company. Accordingly, the positioning statement aims to provide a shared view of the offering's strategy to all relevant entities in the company.

In addition to informing different company entities about the offering's strategy, the positioning statement has an important part in ensuring that the company's external collaborators — including research and development and product design partners, advertising and public relations agencies, channel partners, and external sales force — correctly understand this strategy. Communicating the offering's strategy to the company's collaborators is particularly important because these entities are typically less familiar with the company's goals and strategic initiatives.

The positioning statement is often confused with an offering's positioning. Although directly related, these concepts reflect different aspects of a company's strategy. An offering's positioning is narrower in scope, focusing on the key aspect of the offering's value proposition. In contrast, the positioning statement has a broader scope and includes not only the offering's positioning but also this offering's target customers.

The positioning statement is also confused with the brand motto and communication tagline. This is because all three capture certain aspects of the offering's strategy. Despite their similarities, however, they have different functions and are written for different audiences. The positioning statement is an internal company document aimed at company employees and collaborators, and is not intended to be seen by customers. In contrast, the brand motto and the communication tagline are explicitly written for the company's customers. Consequently, the brand motto and communication tagline use catchy, memorable phrases designed to capture customers' attention, whereas the positioning statement is written in a straightforward manner with a focus on the logic rather than on the form of expression.

To illustrate, Gillette's positioning statement can be written as: *For all men who shave, Gillette provides the best shaving experience because it uses the most innovative shaving technology.* Gillette's brand motto is much more succinct and memorable: *Gillette. The Best a Man Can Get.* Finally, one of Gillette's communication taglines for its Fusion ProGlide razor highlights a particular aspect of its razor: *Less Tug and Pull.* In the same vein, BMW's positioning statement can be articulated as: *BMW is the best vehicle for drivers who care about performance because it is designed to be the ultimate driving machine.* BMW's brand motto is: *The Ultimate Driving Machine.* A recent advertising tagline is: *BMW. We Make Only One Thing: The Ultimate Driving Machine.*[7]

Depending on the audience, there are three types of positioning statements: the *customer-focused positioning statement*, which articulates the offering's value proposition for target customers; the *collaborator-focused positioning statement*, which articulates the offering's value proposition for the company's collaborators; and the *company-focused positioning statement*, which articulates the offering's value proposition for the company stakeholders. These three types of positioning statements are discussed in more detail in the following sections.

Customer-Focused Positioning Statement

The customer-focused positioning statement is by far the most popular type of positioning statement. A typical customer-focused positioning statement involves three components: *target customers, frame of reference,* and *primary benefit(s).* These three aspects of the positioning statement are outlined below.

- Target customers are buyers for whom the company will tailor its offerings. These customers are defined by the key benefit(s) they seek to receive from the offering as well as by their demographic and/or behavioral profile. The selection of target customers is discussed in more detail in Chapter 4.

- The frame of reference identifies the reference point used to define the offering. The frame of reference can be either noncomparative or comparative. *Noncomparative* framing relates the value of the offering to the customer need it aims to fulfill without explicitly comparing it to other offerings; in contrast, *comparative* framing defines the offering by contrasting it to other offerings. The selection of a frame of reference is discussed in more detail in Chapter 5.

- The **primary benefit** identifies the primary reason why customers will consider, buy, and use the offering. The primary benefit typically highlights the key value driver(s) defining the worth of the offering for target customers. The primary benefit could also involve justification of why the offering can claim this benefit. The selection of the primary benefit is discussed in more detail in Chapter 5.

The customer-focused positioning statement is a blueprint of the way(s) in which the company will create customer value. Accordingly, the core question the customer-focused positioning statement must answer is: *Who are the offering's target customers and why would they buy and use the company's offering?*

The organization and the key components of a customer-focused positioning statement can be illustrated with the following examples.

Example A (Noncomparative Positioning): For [target customers][offering] offers [frame of reference] that is [primary benefit] because [justification of the benefit].

For the tradesman who uses power tools to make a living, DeWalt offers dependable professional tools that are engineered to be tough and are backed by a guarantee of repair or replacement within 48 hours.

Example A (Comparative Positioning): For [target customers][offering] offers [frame of reference] that is more [primary benefit] than [competition] because [justification of the benefit].

For the tradesman who uses power tools to make a living, DeWalt offers professional tools that are more dependable than any other brand because they are engineered to be tough and are backed by a guarantee of repair or replacement within 48 hours.

Example B (Noncomparative Positioning): For [target customers][offering] is the [frame of reference] that provides the best [primary benefit] because [justification of the benefit].

For all men who shave, Gillette Fusion is the razor that provides the best shaving experience because it uses the most innovative shaving technology.

Example B (Comparative Positioning): For [target customers][offering] is the [frame of reference] that provides [primary benefit] than [competition] because [justification of the benefit].

For all men who shave, Gillette Fusion is the razor that provides a better shaving experience than Mach 3 because it has the latest shaving technology.

Example C (Noncomparative Positioning): [Offering] is the [frame of reference] that gives [target customers][primary benefit] because [justification of the benefit].

Mountain Dew is the soft drink that gives young, active consumers who have little time for sleep the energy they need because it has a very high level of caffeine.

Example C (Comparative Positioning): [Offering] is the [frame of reference] that gives [target customers] more [primary benefit] than [competition] because [justification of the benefit].

Mountain Dew is the soft drink that gives young, active consumers who have little time for sleep more energy than any other brand because it has a very high level of caffeine.

Example D (Noncomparative Positioning): [Offering] is a good [frame of reference] for [target customers] because [primary benefit].

Gatorade is a good source of hydration for athletes because it rehydrates, replenishes, and refuels.

Example D (Comparative Positioning): [Offering] is a better [frame of reference] for [target customers] than [competition] because [primary benefit].

Gatorade is a better source of hydration for athletes because it rehydrates, replenishes, and refuels in ways that water can't.

Collaborator-Focused Positioning Statement

Creating value for target customers, although important, is only one aspect of ensuring an offering's success. To succeed, an offering has to create value not only for its target customers but also for the company's collaborators. Accordingly, in addition to developing a customer-focused positioning statement, managers need to develop a positioning statement outlining the offering's value for its collaborators.

The collaborator-focused positioning statement is similar to the customer-focused positioning statement, with the main difference that instead of identifying target customers and the key aspects of the offering's value proposition for these customers, it identifies the company's key collaborators and delineates the key aspects of the offering's value proposition for these collaborators. The key question the collaborator-focused positioning statement must answer is: *Who are the offering's key collaborators and why would they support the company's offering?*

The typical collaborator-focused positioning statement consists of three key components: *collaborators, the frame of reference, and the primary benefit.* The overall structure of the collaborator-focused positioning statement is similar to the structure of the customer-focused statement. Examples of collaborator-focused positioning statements are shown below.

Example A (Noncomparative Positioning): [Offering][frame of reference] is an excellent choice for [collaborators] because [primary benefit].

DeWalt power tools are a great choice for retailers because they are profitable.

Example A (Comparative Positioning): [Offering][frame of reference] is a better choice for [collaborators] than [competition] because [primary benefit].

DeWalt power tools are a better choice for retailers than Makita because they offer price protection from discount retailers.

Example B (Noncomparative Positioning): For [collaborators] who seek [primary benefit], [offering] is an excellent [product category] because [justification of the benefit].

For mass-market retailers who seek to grow profits, Gillette Fusion offers a consumer staple that will generate high profit margins.

Example B (Comparative Positioning): For [collaborators] who seek [primary benefit], [offering] is a better [frame of reference] than [competition] because [justification of the benefit].

> For mass-market retailers who seek to grow sales revenues and market share, Gillette Fusion offers a consumer staple that will generate higher profit margins than Gillette Mach3.

Company-Focused Positioning Statement

Creating value for target customers and collaborators, although important, is not sufficient to ensure the market success of an offering. To succeed, an offering must also create value for the company. Therefore, in addition to developing a positioning statement outlining the offering's value for target customers and collaborators, managers need to outline the offering's value for the company.

The company-focused positioning statement identifies the company's strategic business unit managing the offering and outlines its key value proposition for the business unit and the company. The company-focused positioning statement aims to justify the viability of the offering to senior management and the key stakeholders (e.g., company directors) by articulating how the offering will help the company achieve its goals. The key question this positioning statement must answer is: *Why should the business unit and the company invest in this offering?*

A typical company-focused positioning statement consists of three key components: *the company, the frame of reference,* and *the primary benefit.* The overall structure of the company-focused positioning statement is similar to the structure of the customer-focused statement. Examples of company-focused positioning statements are shown below.

Example A (Noncomparative Positioning): [Offering] is an excellent [frame of reference] for [company] because [the primary benefit derived from the offering].

> DeWalt power tools are an excellent choice for Black & Decker because they offer high profit margins.

Example A (Comparative Positioning): [Offering] is a better [frame of reference] for [company] than [alternative options] because [primary benefit].

> DeWalt power tools are a better strategic option for Black & Decker than Black & Decker Professional power tools because they have a larger margin and generate greater sales volume.

Example B (Noncomparative Positioning): [Offering] is an excellent choice for [company] because [the primary benefit derived from the offering].

> Fusion is an excellent option for Gillette because it will assert Gillette's position as the leader in the wet-shaving market and will ensure high profit margins.

Example B (Comparative Positioning): [Offering] is the [frame of reference] that gives [company] greater [primary benefit] than [alternative options] because [justification of the benefit].

Fusion is the wet-shaving system that gives Gillette greater market share than Mach3 because it has higher profit margins.

DEVELOPING A COMMUNICATION PLAN

Advertising says to people, "Here's what we've got.
Here's what it will do for you. Here's how to get it."
—Leo Burnett, the founder of Leo Burnett advertising agency

The communication plan outlines the ways in which the company will inform the relevant market entities—target customers, collaborators, and/or the company employees and stakeholders—about the specific attributes of its offering(s). The logic of the organization of the communication plan and its key aspects are the focus of this chapter.

The Communication Plan as a Component of the Marketing Plan

The communication plan builds on the strategic marketing plan to articulate in greater detail the specifics of the offering's communication. The key difference is that instead of addressing all aspects of the offering, as in the marketing plan, the communication plan focuses only on the communication aspects of the offering and only briefly outlines the other aspects of the marketing plan (usually in the situation overview section of the plan) to provide the background for the proposed communication campaign.

The need for a separate communication plan is driven by a practical consideration: to provide managers responsible for the offering's communication (e.g., advertising, public relations, and social media agencies) with a focused and concise document to guide communication decisions. Accordingly, the communication plan typically begins with an overview of the overall marketing plan and then zeroes in on the communication aspects of the offering to delineate the specifics of a particular communication campaign.

A company's communication activities are delineated in a communication plan that follows a structure mirroring the organization of the marketing plan outlined in Chapter 3. The communication plan starts with an executive summary, followed by a situation analysis; it then sets a goal, formulates a communication strategy, delineates the tactical aspects of the company's communication, articulates a plan to implement the specific communication activities, defines a set of controls to monitor the progress of the communication campaign, and concludes with a set of relevant exhibits. The key elements of the communication plan are illustrated in Figure 1.

Figure 1. The Communication Plan

Executive Summary		
What are the key aspects of the company's communication campaign?		

Situation Overview		
Company What are the company history, culture, resources, offerings, and ongoing activities?		**Market** What are the key aspects of the markets in which the company competes?

Goal		
Focus What is the focus of the company's communication?		**Benchmarks** What are the temporal and quantitative benchmarks for reaching the goal?

Strategy		
Audience Who is the company's target audience?		**Message** What is the message the company aims to communicate?

Tactics		
Media Where will the audience encounter the company's communication?		**Creative** How will the company's message be expressed?

Implementation		
Development What resources need to be developed/acquired to communicate the company's message?		**Deployment** What is the process of bringing the company's message to the target audience?

Control		
Performance How will the company evaluate the effectiveness of the communication campaign?		**Environment** How will the company monitor the environment to identify emerging opportunities and threats?

Exhibits		
What are the details/evidence supporting the company's communication plan?		

Because the ultimate goal of the communication plan is to guide a company's actions, the G-STIC component (goal, strategy, tactics, implementation, and control) is the focal aspect of the communication plan. The other elements of the communication plan—the executive summary, situation overview, and exhibits—aim to facilitate an understanding of the logic underlying the communication plan and provide specifics of the proposed course of action. A detailed outline of the key components of a communication plan for launching a new campaign is discussed in more detail in the following sections.

The Key Components of the Communication Plan

The communication plan comprises eight key components: *executive summary, situation overview, goal, strategy, tactics, implementation, control,* and *exhibits*.

Executive Summary

The executive summary offers an overview of the key aspects of the communication plan. It typically includes the relevant aspects of the goal, strategy, tactics, implementation, and control components of the communication plan. The aim of the executive summary is to provide the reader with an outline of the key aspects of the communication plan.

Situation Overview

The situation overview section of the communication plan aims to provide the relevant context in which the offering operates and ensure consistency between the communication plan and the overall marketing plan. The situation overview section typically consists of two parts: *market overview* and *offering overview.*

- The market overview summarizes the key aspects of the market in which the communication takes place. The market overview typically follows the 5-C framework (customers, competitors, collaborators, company, and context) to provide an overview of the target market and identify the key factors that are likely to influence communication decisions.

- The offering overview outlines the aspects of the market offering (product, service, brand, price, incentives, communication, and distribution) that are likely to be relevant in developing the offering's communication campaign.

Goal

The goal section of the communication plan defines the desired outcomes of the communication campaign. Defining the communication goal involves two components: *focus* and *benchmarks.*

- Goal focus outlines the key outcome(s) that the company aims to achieve with the communication campaign. Common communication goal foci can include creating awareness, generating interest, strengthening preferences, and inciting action.

- Performance benchmarks quantify the desired outcome by defining a particular level that needs to be achieved and establishing a time frame for achieving this outcome.

For example, the communication goal might involve creating top-of-mind awareness (goal focus) of the company's new product among 20% of young adults in urban areas (quantitative benchmark) prior to product launch (temporal benchmark).

Strategy

The communication strategy follows directly from the offering's overall marketing strategy and comprises two key components: *target audience* and the *message* to be communicated.

- The target audience identifies the recipients of the communication campaign. An offering's target audience is not limited to its target customers. In addition to target customers, the target audience can include buyers, influencers, collaborators, company employees, company stakeholders, and society at large.

- The **message** defines the information that will be communicated and the value that this information will create for the relevant market entities. The message can involve one or more attributes of the offering: product, service, brand, price, incentives, and distribution. Thus, product- and service-related messages inform the target audience of the characteristics of the company's products and services; brand-related messages focus on the identity and the meaning of the company's or offering's brand; price-related messages communicate the offering's price; incentives-related messages communicate the incentives associated with the offering, such as sales promotions, volume discounts, and bonus offers; and distribution-related messages highlight the offering's availability in distribution channels.

Tactics

Communication tactics identify the *media* and the *creative* means used to convey the message to the target audience.

- The **media** defines the means used by the company to convey its message to the target audience. Based on the entity initiating the communication, media can be divided into two types: *outbound* and *inbound*. Outbound media involves communication initiated by the company. The most common forms of outbound media include advertising, public relations, social media, direct marketing, personal selling, event sponsorship, product placement, product-based communication, and product samples and free trials. Inbound media involves communication initiated by the public rather than the company. Common types of inbound media include online search, personal interaction, phone, online forums, email, and mail.

- The **creative** aspect of communication identifies the specific approach (e.g., the specific text and imagery) used to convey the chosen message. The development of the creative solution involves two key decisions: *message appeal* and *execution format*. Message appeal reflects the approach used to communicate the company's message. Most creative solutions involve at least one of two types of appeals: information-based and emotion-based. Execution format is the specific method used to convey a particular appeal using the means of the selected media format. Because different types of media tend to utilize different creative means, creative solutions often vary depending on the media chosen.

Implementation

The implementation defines the process of making the communication strategy and tactics a market reality. Specifically, the implementation aspect of the communication plan involves *developing the resources needed to implement the plan, developing the actual communication campaign*, and *deploying this campaign in the target market*.

- **Resource development** involves ensuring the resources necessary to run the communication campaign. This can involve recruiting talent (creative team, research team, actors/spokespeople), identifying collaborators (advertising, public relations, and online agencies; media partners; co-promoters), and securing the financial resources for the campaign.

- **Campaign development** involves securing the relevant media (air time in audio-visual media outlets; advertising space in print, online, and outdoor outlets) and creating the communication (e.g., commercials, print advertisements, online banners, and other offering-related content) that will be shared with the target audience.

- **Commercial deployment** involves launching the communication campaign in the target market. This involves airing the commercials, placing the advertisements in the different media outlets, publishing the developed content, and bidding on relevant keywords to ensure high ranking in paid search results.

Control

The control section of the communication plan identifies the ways in which the company will ensure adequate implementation of the communication plan. Specifically, the control section addresses two issues: *measuring communication effectiveness* and *monitoring the communication environment*.

- **Measuring communication effectiveness** aims to ensure adequate progress toward the communication goal. To this end, this section of the communication plan defines the ways in which communication performance is measured (e.g., key performance metrics) and identifies the processes by which performance evaluation is implemented.

- **Monitoring the environment** aims to ensure that the communication plan is relevant in the face of the changing market environment. Specifically, this section of the communication plan identifies the processes involved in gathering market intelligence to identify communication opportunities and threats.

Exhibits

The exhibit section offers additional details in the form of tables, charts, and appendices that support the communication plan. Common communication exhibits include: a communication budget, a communication schedule, an advertising plan, a public relations plan, a social media plan, a mobile communication plan, an inbound communication plan, and a methodology for measuring communication effectiveness.

DEVELOPING MEANINGFUL EXHIBITS

A picture shows me at a glance what it
takes dozens of pages of a book to explain.
—Ivan Turgenev, Russian
novelist and playwright

E xhibits provide detailed information concerning a particular aspect of the marketing plan. Despite their importance to the ability of the marketing plan to achieve its goal—guide the company's actions and inform the relevant market entities about the specifics of the company's offering—managers often view exhibits as an afterthought rather than as an integral component of the marketing plan. The purpose of this note, therefore, is to outline the key principles of creating meaningful exhibits that enhance the logic and add clarity to the marketing plan.

Choosing the Right Content

The main purpose of exhibits is to effectively communicate relevant information. Therefore, the effectiveness of an exhibit depends on the degree to which it facilitates an understanding of the rationale and the specifics of the marketing plan. Accordingly, effective exhibits should be *necessary, specific, clear, succinct, and stylistically functional*.

- **Necessary.** Exhibits must present information that is relevant to the set goal and the proposed course of action.

- **Specific.** Because exhibits illustrate a specific point made in the text, they should be related to the main text contained in the body of the plan and each exhibit should be referenced in the main text.

- **Clear.** Exhibits should be self-contained so that the reader can understand their meaning without necessarily referring to the main text. To this end, exhibits should have a title.

- **Succinct.** Exhibits should contain only information that is directly relevant to the specific point they aim to make.

- **Stylistically functional.** The functionality of an exhibit should supersede its style. To this end, exhibits should avoid visually distracting details and be stylistically consistent with the other exhibits in the text.

Deciding on the Right Format

Depending on their format, most exhibits fall into one of three types: tables, charts, and appendices.

- **Tables** typically show exact numerical values arranged in columns and rows to aid comparison. Tables allow for the efficient presentation of large amounts of data and are often used for market research and financial data.
- **Figures** involve any type of illustration other than a table. A figure may be a graph, chart, photograph, drawing, or other illustration. Each figure should make a specific point and should be clear and informative on its own.
- **Appendices** provide detailed information about a specific issue that would be distracting to read in the main body of the plan. Appendices can contain tables, figures, or text and are used for peripherally related and/or extremely detailed data.

Organizing the Exhibits

Exhibits must be developed in a way that facilitates understanding. To this end, most exhibits include the following components: *label, title, outline, body, notes*, and *source*.

- The **label** indicates the type of exhibit (e.g., table, figure, or appendix) and, when appropriate, an enumeration.
- The **title** describes the essence of the exhibit, that is, what this exhibit aims to demonstrate.
- The **outline** presents the key point(s) made by the exhibit.
- The **body** of the exhibit contains the core information conveyed by the exhibit.
- The **note** includes various information that helps the reader gain a better understanding of the exhibit (e.g., the assumptions made in developing the exhibit).
- The **source** indicates the origin of the factual information used in the exhibit.

Figure 1: Organizing the Information Presented as a Table

Label ⇒ **Exhibit**

Title ⇒ **Price Elasticity Analysis**

Outline ⇒ Price and Cross-Price Elasticities of Coke, Pepsi, and RC Cola in Market X

Body ⇒

Brand	Coke	Pepsi	RC Cola
Coke	-1.9	0.4	0.8
Pepsi	0.4	-2.2	0.7
RC Cola	0.2	0.2	-3.1 ⇐ **Emphasis**

Note ⇒ Note: Cell numbers indicate the percentage change in sales volume resulting from a percentage change in price. Diagonal cells indicate a brand's own price elasticity. Off-diagonal cells indicate the effect of price change of brands listed in the top row on sales volume of brands listed in the first column.

Source ⇒ Source: Proprietary data

Figure 2: Organizing the Information Presented as a Figure

Because most exhibits aim to illustrate and/or support a particular point in the marketing plan, they often benefit from focusing a reader's attention on a specific aspect of the available information, such as a particular data point (Figure 1) and the magnitude of change (Figure 2).

Using Figures as Exhibits

Because figures present information in an easy-to-comprehend visual format, they are frequently used in developing marketing plans. Some of the most common figure types include *line charts, column charts, bar charts, pie charts, matrices, positioning maps, flowcharts,* and *organizational charts.*

Line Chart

A line chart is one of the most popular types of figure. It is the easiest to draw, the most compact, and the clearest figure type for discerning whether a trend is increasing, decreasing, fluctuating, or remaining constant (Figure 3).

Figure 3. Line Chart

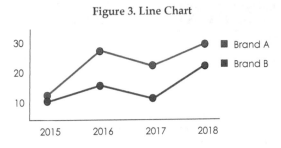

Column Chart

A column chart emphasizes levels or magnitudes and is more suitable for data on activities that occur within a set period of time. There are three common types of column charts (Figure 4). *Single-column charts* show changes in magnitude of an item as a function of a particular factor, most often time. *Grouped-column charts* show the relationships among two or more items as a function of a particular factor. *Subdivided charts* are used to show components of a whole as either an actual value or a percentage.

Figure 4. Column Charts

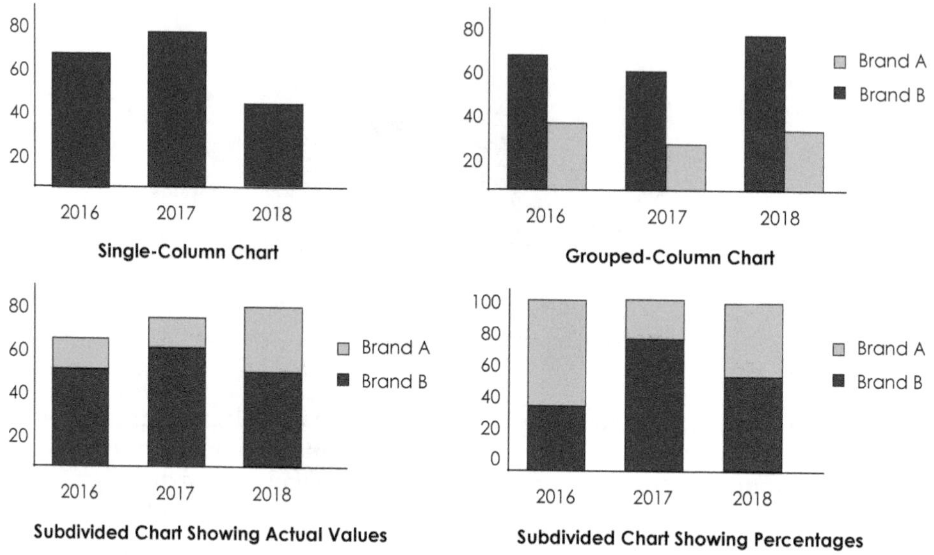

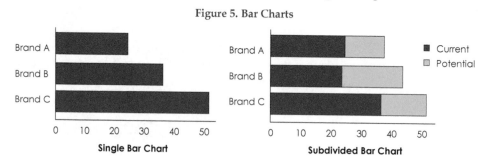

Single-Column Chart

Grouped-Column Chart

Subdivided Chart Showing Actual Values

Subdivided Chart Showing Percentages

Bar Chart

A bar chart is similar to a column chart, except it typically compares data across categories rather than across time (Figure 5). Depending on the type of data, bar charts can involve a single bar or a subdivided bar that includes multiple data points.

Figure 5. Bar Charts

Single Bar Chart

Subdivided Bar Chart

Pie Chart

A pie chart is a visual representation of information showing parts as a proportion of the whole. Pie charts commonly represent factors such as market share and customer segments that are mutually exclusive and collectively exhaustive (Figure 6). To illustrate the composition of a particular segment, the bar of pie chart subdivides one section of the pie into a 100% column chart.

Figure 6. Pie Chart

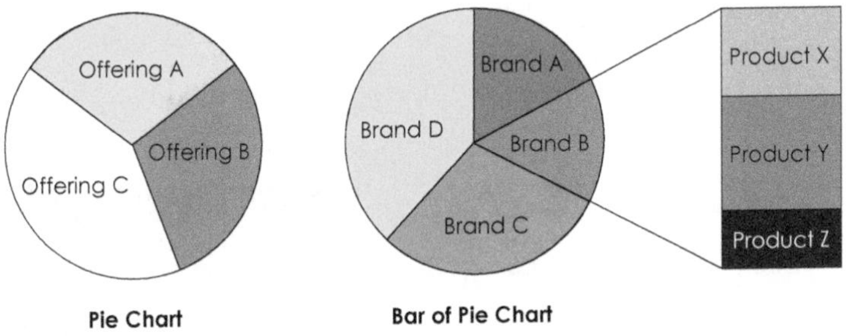

Pie Chart

Bar of Pie Chart

Matrix

Matrices are a common tool for organizing qualitative data given by two or more variables. Matrices are particularly useful in cases where the outcome of one of the variables is
a function of the value of the other variable. The simplest and perhaps most popular matrix form is the 2 x 2 matrix composed of two variables, each with two levels (Figure 7).

Figure 7. A 2 x 2 Matrix

	Current customers	New customers
Current products	Market penetration	Market development
New products	Product development	Diversification

Perceptual Map

A perceptual map offers a spatial representation of the perceived relationships among
products, services, or companies (Figure 8). Perceptual maps can have any number of
dimensions. The two-dimensional maps are the most common and are the easiest to in-
terpret, whereas the more complex multi-attribute perceptual maps provide a deeper understanding of people's preferences. In addition to plotting the available offerings, perceptual maps can also display consumers' ideal points, which reflect customers' ideal
combinations of different aspects of the offering. Because they are often used to illustrate
an offering's positioning, perceptual maps are also referred to as positioning maps.

Figure 8. Perceptual Map

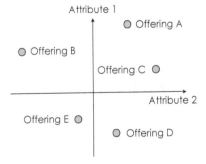

Flowchart

Flowcharts visualize and add structure to business processes, making them easier to explain and understand. Flowcharts are typically used to graphically represent the main steps in a process and the relationship between individual components (Figure 9).

Figure 9. Flowchart

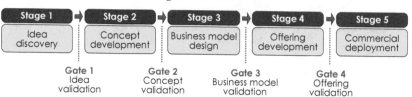

Project-Management Chart

Project-management charts illustrate the logistics of managing a particular project. A common approach to developing project-management charts lists all the tasks to be performed on the vertical axis and presents a timeline for completing each task on the horizontal axis (Figure 10). In cases when individual tasks are assigned to different teams, horizontal bars also represent the allocation of tasks across teams.

Figure 10. Project-Management Chart

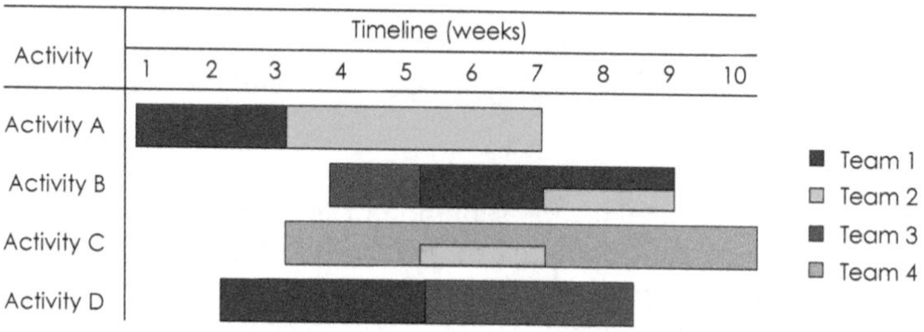

Organizational Chart

An organizational chart is a diagram representing the internal structure of an organization and the relationships among its components (Figure 11). In addition to the functional responsibilities, organizational charts might also include the name and the position of the key employees in each organizational unit.

Figure 11. Functional Organizational Chart

PERFORMANCE METRICS AND ANALYSES

> *Not everything that can be counted counts,*
> *and not everything that counts can be counted.*
> — Albert Einstein, theoretical physicist

Performance metrics are an important aspect of defining the goal and control aspects of the company's marketing plan. Thus, when setting the goal, a company must define the particular metric(s), such as net income, market share, or sales volume, that it aims to achieve with its offering. In the same vein, the control aspect of the marketing plan must define the metric(s) on which the company's performance will be assessed. The key performance metrics and the related analyses are outlined in the following sections.

Performance Metrics

Performance metrics enable the company to monitor its progress toward its goals. Based on their focus, most performance metrics can be divided into three categories: *company metrics*, which are directly related to the ultimate goal the company aims to achieve; *customer metrics*, which capture customer response to the company's actions; and *marketing mix metrics*, which depict the performance of the company's offering on key attributes: product, service, brand, price, incentives, communication, and distribution. These three types of performance metrics are outlined below.

Company Metrics

Compound Annual Growth Rate (CAGR): The year-to-year growth rate of an investment during a specified period.

Gross (Profit) Margin: The ratio of gross (total) profit to gross (total) revenue. Gross margin analysis is a useful tool because it implicitly includes unit selling prices of products or services, unit costs, and unit volume. Gross margin is different from contribution margin (discussed later): Contribution margin includes all variable costs, whereas gross margin includes some, but often not all, variable costs, a number of which can be part of the operating margin.

$$\text{Gross margin} = \frac{\text{Gross profit}}{\text{Gross revenue}} = \frac{\text{Gross revenue} - \text{Cost of goods sold}}{\text{Gross revenue}}$$

Gross Profit: The difference between gross (total) revenue and total cost of goods sold. Gross profit can also be calculated on a per-unit basis as the difference between unit selling price and unit cost of goods sold. For example, if a company sells 100 units, each priced at $1 and each costing the company $.30 to manufacture, then the unit gross profit is $.70, the total gross profit is $70, and the unit and total gross margins are 70%.

$$\text{Gross profit}_{Total} = \text{Revenue}_{Total} - \text{Cost of goods sold}_{Total}$$

$$\text{Gross profit}_{Unit} = \text{Price}_{Unit} - \text{Cost of goods sold}_{Unit}$$

Gross Revenue: Total receipts from a company's business activities.

Income Statement: The income statement (also referred to as the *profit and loss statement*) is a financial document showing a company's income and expenses during a given period. It typically identifies revenues, costs, operating expenses, operating income, and earnings (Figure 1).

Figure 1: The Income (Profit and Loss) Statement

Gross Revenues	
Sales revenues	$ 18,000
Returns and allowances	(3,000)
Total (Gross) Revenues	15,000
Cost of Goods Sold	
Product costs	(4,500)
Services costs	(1,500)
Total Cost of Goods Sold	(6,000)
Gross Profit	9,000
Gross Margin	60%
Operating Expenses	
Sales and marketing	5,000
General and administrative	1,000
Research and development	1,500
Total Operating Expenses	7,500
Operating Income	1,500
Operating Margin	10%
Other Revenues (Expenses)	
Interest expense	(250)
Depreciation and amortization	(100)
Income tax expense	(400)
Total Other Revenues (Expenses)	(750)
Net Income (Earnings)	750
Net (Profit) Margin	5%

Internal Rate of Return (IRR): The annualized effective compounded return rate that can be earned on the invested capital (i.e., yield on investment).

Market Share: An offering's share of the total sales of all offerings within the product category in which the brand competes. Market share is determined by dividing an offering's sales volume by the total category sales volume. Sales can be defined in terms of revenues or on a unit basis (e.g., number of items sold or number of customers served).

$$\text{Market share} = \frac{\text{An offering's sales in a given market}}{\text{Total sales in a given market}}$$

Net Earnings: See *net income.*

Net Income: Gross revenue minus all costs and expenses (cost of goods sold, operating expenses, depreciation, interest, and taxes) during a given period of time.

$$\text{Net income} = \text{Gross revenue} - \text{Total costs}$$

Net Margin: The ratio of net income to gross (total) revenue.

$$\text{Net margin} = \frac{\text{Net income}}{\text{Gross revenue}}$$

Operating Expenses: The primary costs, other than cost of goods sold, incurred to generate revenues (e.g., sales, marketing, research and development, and general and administrative expenses).

Operating Income: Gross profit minus operating expenses. Operating income reflects the firm's profitability from current operations without regard to the interest charges accruing from the firm's capital structure.

$$\text{Operating income} = \text{Gross profit} - \text{Operating expenses}$$

Operating Margin: The ratio of operating income to gross (total) revenue.

$$\text{Operating margin} = \frac{\text{Operating income}}{\text{Gross revenue}}$$

Return on Investment (ROI): Net income as a percentage of the investment required for generating this income.

$$\text{ROI} = \frac{\text{Gain from an investment} - \text{Cost of investment}}{\text{Cost of investment}}$$

Return on Marketing Investment (ROMI): A measure of the efficiency of a company's marketing expenditures, most often calculated in terms of incremental net income, sales revenues, market share, or contribution margin. ROMI can also be calculated with respect to the overall marketing expenditures or to a specific marketing mix variable (e.g., branding, incentives, or communication).

$$\text{ROMI} = \frac{\text{Incremental net income generated by the marketing investment}}{\text{Cost of the marketing investment}}$$

Return on Sales (ROS): Net income as a percentage of sales revenues.

$$\text{ROS} = \frac{\text{Net income}}{\text{Sales revenue}}$$

Customer Metrics

Brand Development Index (BDI): A measure of the degree to which sales of a given offering (or a product line associated with a particular brand) have captured the total market potential in a particular geographic area. BDI quantifies the sales potential of a given brand in a particular market.

$$BDI = \frac{\text{Percent of an offering's total sales in market X}}{\text{Percent of the total population in market X}}$$

Category Development Index (CDI): A measure of the degree to which sales in a given category have captured the total market potential in a particular geographic area. CDI quantifies the sales potential of a given category in a particular market.

$$CDI = \frac{\text{Percent of a category's total sales in market X}}{\text{Percent of the total population in market X}}$$

Conversion Rate: The number of potential customers who have tried the offering relative to the total number of customers aware of the offering.

$$\text{Conversion rate} = \frac{\text{Current and former customers}}{\text{Potential customers aware of the offering}}$$

Customer Attrition Rate (Churn Rate): The number of customers who discontinue using a company's offering during a specified period relative to the average total number of customers during that same period.

$$\text{Attrition rate} = \frac{\text{Number of customers who disadopt an offering}}{\text{Total number of customers}}$$

Customer Equity: The monetary and strategic value customers are likely to create for the company during their tenure with this company. Customer equity goes beyond the current profitability of a customer to include the entire stream of profits (adjusted for the time value of money) that a company is likely to receive from this customer. A customer can create value for the company in at least three different ways: (1) by directly generating revenues (and profits) for the company through purchase of the company's products and services (direct value), (2) by promoting the company's products and services to other buyers (communication value), and (3) by providing the company with information that can help increase the effectiveness and efficiency of its operations (information value).

Penetration Rate: The number of customers who have tried the offering at least once relative to the total number of potential customers.

$$\text{Penetration rate} = \frac{\text{Current and former customers}}{\text{Potential customers}}$$

Retention Rate: The number of customers who have purchased the offering during the current buying cycle (month, quarter, or year) relative to the number of customers who purchased the offering during the last cycle. Also used in reference to the number of customers who have repurchased the offering relative to the total number of customers who have tried the product at least once.

$$\text{Retention rate} = \frac{\text{Active customers during the current period}}{\text{Active customers during the last period}}$$

Product and Service Metrics

Net Promoter Score: A popular metric designed to measure customers' preference for a company's products and services.[8] The basic idea is fairly simple: A company's current and potential customers are asked to indicate the likelihood that they will recommend the company's product or service to another person (e.g., "How likely is it that you would recommend this product/service to a friend or colleague?"). Responses are typically scored on a 0–10 scale, with 0 meaning extremely unlikely and 10 meaning extremely likely. Based on their responses, customers are divided into one of three categories: promoters (those with ratings of 9 or 10), passives (those with ratings of 7 or 8), and detractors (those with ratings of 6 or lower). The net promoter score is then calculated as the difference between the percentage of a company's promoters and detractors. For example, if 40% of a company's customers are classified as promoters and 25% are classified as detractors, the company's net promoter score is 15%.

Product/Service Preferences: A measure of the degree to which a product/service appeals to current and potential customers. Preferences can be measured in absolute terms (i.e., independent from the other products and services in the marketplace) or relative to other offerings (e.g., the degree to which the company's products and services are perceived to be better than competitors' products and services). Preferences typically comprise two dimensions: the valence of preferences (e.g., positive vs. negative) and the strength of preferences (e.g., strong vs. weak). Product and service preferences can be measured using a variety of techniques, such as questionnaires, conjoint analysis, and perceptual maps.

Product/Service Satisfaction: A measure of customers' experience with a product. Unlike product-preference metrics that can be measured prior to purchase as well as after purchase, satisfaction requires consumers to have actual experience with the product or service. Satisfaction is typically measured using a five-point or a seven-point scale (e.g., very dissatisfied, somewhat dissatisfied, neither satisfied nor dissatisfied, somewhat satisfied, and very satisfied).

Purchase Intent: Self-reported likelihood of purchasing a company's products or services. A popular approach to estimating the purchase likelihood involves using a five-point scale with the following anchors: "definitely would buy," "probably would buy," "might or might not buy," "probably would not buy," and "definitely would not buy." To account for an overestimation bias, whereby respondents tend to overestimate the probability of actually purchasing the surveyed product, the stated purchase probabilities are typically corrected. A common methodology for correcting this overestimation bias involves using generalized industry estimates. To illustrate, responses involving consumer packaged goods are sometimes corrected as follows: "definitely would buy" responses are reduced by 20 percent (which implies that only 80 percent of those stating that they will definitely buy the product actually end up buying it); "probably would buy" responses are reduced by 70 percent (which implies that only 30 percent of those stating that they will probably buy the product actually end up buying it); and responses falling into the three remaining categories are considered to be no-purchase responses.

Brand Metrics

Brand Power reflects the impact of the brand on the market response to the offering. A brand has greater power if market entities (e.g., customers and collaborators) react more favorably to an offering when they are aware of the brand name. To illustrate, one of the benefits of brand power is the price premium customers are willing to pay for the branded product compared to an identical unbranded product. In addition to the price premium, other dimensions of brand power include greater customer loyalty; enhanced perception of product performance; greater licensing, merchandising, and brand extension opportunities; less vulnerability to service inconsistencies and marketing crises;

more elastic response to price decreases and more inelastic response to price increases; greater communication effectiveness; and increased channel power.

Brand Equity is the (monetary) value of the brand to the company. Unlike brand power, which reflects the value a brand creates in the minds of customers, brand equity reflects the value of the brand to the company. Brand equity is a function of brand power as well as the company's utilization of the power of its brand, reflected in its user base, sales volume, and pricing. Common approaches to measuring brand equity include (1) calculating brand equity based on the costs for building the brand at the time of valuation (cost-based approach); (2) calculating brand equity based on the difference in the cash flows generated from the branded product and a functionally equivalent but unbranded product, adjusted for the costs of creating the brand (market-based approach); and (3) calculating brand equity based on the net present value of the cash flows derived from the brand's future earnings (financial approach).

Price and Incentives Metrics

Cross-Price Elasticity: The percentage change in quantity sold of a given offering caused by a percentage change in the price of another offering.

Incentives Ratio: Percentage of sales that involves incentives relative to the company's total sales.

$$\text{Incentives ratio} = \frac{\text{Sales revenues with incentives}}{\text{Total sales revenues}}$$

Pass-Through Incentives Ratio: Percentage of the incentives provided to customers by a given channel member (e.g., a retailer) relative to the incentives provided to that channel member (e.g., by a manufacturer).

$$\text{Pass-through incentives ratio} = \frac{\text{Incentives provided to customers by a channel member}}{\text{Incentives provided to the channel member}}$$

Price Elasticity: The percentage change in quantity sold ($\Delta Q\%$) relative to the percentage change in price ($\Delta P\%$) for a given product or service. Because in most cases the quantity demanded decreases when the price increases, this ratio is negative; however, for practical purposes, the absolute value of the ratio is used, and price elasticity is often reported as a positive number.

$$E_p = \frac{\Delta Q\%}{\Delta P\%} = \frac{\Delta Q \cdot P}{\Delta P \cdot Q}$$

To illustrate, a price elasticity of –2 means that a 5% price increase will result in a 10% decrease in the quantity sold. In cases where (the absolute value of) price elasticity is greater than 1, demand is said to be elastic, meaning that a change in price causes a larger change in quantity demanded. In contrast, when (the absolute value of) price elasticity is less than 1, demand is said to be inelastic, meaning that a change in price results in a smaller change in quantity demanded. When (the absolute value of) price elasticity is equal to 1, demand is said to be unitary, meaning that a change in price results in an equal change in quantity demanded. Because price elasticity reflects proportional changes, it does not depend on the units in which the price and quantity are expressed. Furthermore, because price elasticity is a function of the initial values, the same absolute changes in price can lead to different price elasticity values at different price points. For example, the volume decline resulting from lowering the price by five cents might be 5% when the initial price is $5.00 but only 1% when the initial price is $1.00.

Communication Metrics

Advertising Awareness: The number of potential customers who are aware of the offering. Awareness is a function of the total volume of advertising delivered to the target audience and the number of exposures necessary to create awareness. In cases where a single exposure is sufficient to create awareness, the awareness level equals the advertising reach.

$$\text{Awareness} = \frac{\text{Reach} \cdot \text{Frequency}}{\text{Number of exposures needed to create awareness}}$$

Advertising Frequency: The number of times the target audience is exposed to an advertisement in a given period. Also used in reference to the number of times an advertisement is repeated through a specific medium during a specific period.

Advertising Reach: The size of the audience that has been exposed to a particular advertisement at least once in a given period (multiple viewings by the same audience do not increase reach). Reach can be stated either as an absolute number or as a fraction of a population. For example, if 40,000 of 100,000 different households are exposed to a given commercial at least once, the reach is 40%.

Awareness Rate: The number of potential customers aware of the offering relative to the total number of potential customers. Depending on the manner in which it is measured, two types of awareness are commonly distinguished: aided awareness, in which respondents are provided with the name of the target offering (e.g., "Have you seen any advertisements for Coca-Cola in the past month?"), and unaided awareness, in which respondents are not provided with any offering-specific information (e.g., "Which soft drinks have you seen advertised during the past month?").

Cost Per Point (CPP): Measure used to represent the cost of a communication campaign. CPP is the media cost of reaching one percent (one rating point) of a particular demographic. See also *gross rating point*.

$$\text{CPP} = \frac{\text{Advertising cost}}{\text{GRP}}$$

Cost Per Thousand (CPM): Measure used to represent the cost of a communication campaign. CPM is the cost of reaching 1,000 individuals or households with an advertising message in a given medium (M is the Roman numeral for 1,000). For example, a television commercial that costs $200,000 to air and reaches 10M viewers has a CPM of $20. The popularity of CPM derives in part from its functioning as a good comparative measure of advertising efficiency across different media (e.g., television, print, and Internet).

$$\text{CPM} = \frac{\text{Advertising cost}}{\text{Total impressions}} \cdot 1,000$$

Gross Rating Point (GRP): A measure of the total volume of advertising delivery to the target audience. GRP is equal to the percent of the population reached times the frequency of exposure. To illustrate, if a given advertisement reaches 60% of the households with an average frequency of three times, then the GRP of the media is equal to 180. GRP can also be calculated by dividing gross impressions by the size of the total audience. A single GRP represents 1% of the total audience in a given region.

$$\text{GRP} = \text{Reach} \cdot \text{Frequency}$$

Share of Voice: A company's communication expenditures relative to those of the entire product category.

$$\text{Share of voice} = \frac{\text{Advertising spend for an offering}}{\text{Advertising spend for the category}}$$

Target Rating Point (TRP): A measure of the total volume of advertising delivery to the target audience. TRP is similar to GRP, but its calculation involves using only the target audience (rather than the total audience watching the program) as the base. Thus, a single TRP represents 1% of the targeted viewers in any particular region.

Distribution Metrics

All-Commodity Volume (ACV): A measure of an offering's availability, typically calculated as the total annual volume of the company's offering in a given geographic area relative to the total sales volume of the retailers in that geographic area across all product categories.

$$\text{ACV} = \frac{\text{Total sales of stores carrying the company's offering}}{\text{Total sales of all stores}}$$

Inventory Turnover: The number of times that inventory is replenished, typically calculated as the ratio of annual revenues generated by a given offering to average inventory.

Same-Store Sales: A metric used in the retail industry for measuring sales of stores that have been open for a year or more and have historical data comparing the current year's sales to last year's sales. Same-store sales are a popular metric because it takes store closings and chain expansions out of the mix, indicating the portion of new sales that resulted from sales growth and the portion that resulted from the opening or closing of stores.

Share of Shelf Space: Shelf space allocated to a given offering relative to the total shelf space in a given geographic area.

Trade Margin: The difference between unit selling price and unit cost at each level of a marketing channel.

Performance Analysis

In addition to monitoring specific metrics, evaluating a company's performance can benefit from an in-depth analysis of the company's margins and the break-even sales volume. *Margin analysis* examines the relationships among a company's gross (total) profit, income, and gross (total) revenue (income margins), as well as the relationships between variable and fixed costs associated with a particular offering (contribution margins). *Break-even analysis*, on the other hand, identifies the point at which the benefits and costs associated with a particular action are equal, and beyond which profit occurs. The most common types of break-even analyses are break-even volume of a fixed-cost investment, break-even volume of a price cut, break-even volume of a variable-cost increase, and break-even rate of cannibalization. The two types of performance analysis — margin and break-even — are outlined below.

Margin Analysis

Contribution Margin ($): When expressed in monetary terms ($), contribution margin typically refers to the difference between total revenue and total variable costs. The contribution margin can also be calculated on a per-unit basis as the difference between the unit selling price and the unit variable cost. The per-unit margin, expressed in monetary terms ($), is also referred to as contribution (i.e., the dollar amount that each unit sold "contributes" to the payment of fixed costs).

$$\text{Contribution margin (\$)}_{\text{Total}} = \text{Revenue}_{\text{Total}} - \text{Variable costs}_{\text{Total}}$$

$$\text{Contribution margin (\$)}_{\text{Unit}} = \text{Price}_{\text{Unit}} - \text{Variable costs}_{\text{Unit}}$$

Contribution Margin (%): When expressed in percentages (%), contribution margin typically refers to the ratio of the difference between total revenue and total variable costs to total revenue. Contribution margin can also be expressed as the ratio of unit contribution to unit selling price.

$$\text{Contribution margin (\%)} = \frac{\text{Revenue}_{\text{Total}} - \text{Variable costs}_{\text{Total}}}{\text{Revenue}_{\text{Total}}}$$

$$\text{Contribution margin (\%)} = \frac{\text{Price}_{\text{Unit}} - \text{Variable costs}_{\text{Unit}}}{\text{Price}_{\text{Unit}}}$$

Fixed Costs: Expenses that do not fluctuate with output volume within a relevant period. Typical examples of fixed costs include research-and-development expenses, mass-media advertising expenses, rent, interest on debt, insurance, plant-and-equipment expenses, and salary of permanent full-time workers. Even though their absolute size remains unchanged regardless of output volume, fixed costs become progressively smaller per unit of output as volume increases, a decrease that results from the larger number of output units over which fixed costs are allocated. See also *variable costs*.

Marginal Cost: The cost of producing one extra unit.

Trade Margin: The difference between unit selling price and unit cost at each level of a distribution channel. Trade margins can be expressed in monetary terms or as a percentage (Figure 1). Note that margins are typically calculated based on sales revenue (sales price) rather than based on cost (purchase price).

Figure 1. Calculating Distribution Channel Margins

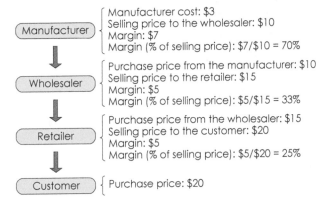

Variable Costs: Expenses that fluctuate in direct proportion to the output volume of units produced. For example, the cost of raw materials and expenses incurred by consumer incentives such as coupons, price discounts, rebates, and premiums, are commonly viewed as variable costs. Other expenses, such as distribution channel incentives and sales force compensation, can be classified as either fixed or variable costs depending on their structure (e.g., fixed salary vs. performance-based compensation). See also *fixed costs*.

Break-Even Analysis

Break-even analysis of a fixed-cost investment identifies the unit or dollar sales volume at which the company is able to recoup a particular investment, such as research-and-development expenses, product improvement costs, and the costs of an advertising campaign. The break-even volume (BEV) of a fixed-cost investment is the ratio of the size of the fixed-cost investment to the unit margin.

$$BEV_{\text{Fixed-cost investment}} = \frac{\text{Fixed-cost investment}}{\text{Unit margin}}$$

To illustrate, consider an offering priced at $100 with variable costs of $50 and fixed costs of $50M. In this case, BEV = $50M/($100 – $50)= 1,000,000. Thus, for a $50M fixed-cost investment to break even, sales volume should reach 1,000,000 items.

Break-even analysis of a price cut estimates the increase in sales volume needed for a price cut to have a neutral impact on profitability. To break even, lost profits resulting from a lower margin after a price cut must be equal to the additional profits generated by the incremental sales volume from the lower price.

$$BEV_{\text{Price cut}} = \frac{\text{Margin}_{\text{Old price}}}{\text{Margin}_{\text{New price}}}$$

To illustrate, consider the impact of a price cut from $100 to $75 for a product with a variable cost of $50. In this case, Margin $_{\text{Old price}}$ = $100 – $50 = $50 and Margin $_{\text{New price}}$ = $75 – $50 = $25. Therefore, BEV $_{\text{Price cut}}$ = $50/$25 = 2. Thus, for the price cut to break even, sales volume should double at the lower price.

Break-even analysis of a variable-cost increase identifies the sales volume at which a company neither makes a profit nor incurs a loss after increasing variable costs. The basic principle of calculating the break-even point of an increase in an offering's variable costs is similar to that of estimating the break-even point of a price cut. The difference is that a decrease in the margin generated by the new offering stems from an increase in the offering's costs rather than a decrease in revenues.

$$BEV_{\text{Variable cost increase}} = \frac{\text{Margin}_{\text{Old variable cost}}}{\text{Margin}_{\text{New variable cost}}}$$

To illustrate, consider the impact of an increase in variable costs from $50 to $60 for a product priced at $100. In this case, Margin $_{\text{Old variable cost}}$ = $100 – $50 = $50 and Margin $_{\text{New variable cost}}$ = $100 – $60 = $40. Therefore, BEV $_{\text{Variable price increase}}$ = $50/$40 = 1.25. Thus, for the variable-cost increase to break even, the ratio of the new to old sales should be 1.25, meaning that sales volume should increase by a factor of .25, or by 25%.

Break-even rate of cannibalization: The maximum proportion of the sales volume of the new offering that can come from the company's existing offering(s) without incurring a loss. The break-even rate (BER) of cannibalization is calculated as the ratio of the cannibalized sales volume of the existing offering to the sales volume generated by the new offering at which a company neither makes a profit nor incurs a loss.

$$BER_{Cannibalization} = \frac{Margin_{New\ Offering}}{Margin_{Old\ Offering}}$$

For example, consider a company launching a new product priced at $70 with variable costs of $60, which cannibalizes the sales of an existing product priced at $100 that also has variable costs of $60. In this case, $Margin_{New\ Offering}$ = $70 – $60 = $10 and $Margin_{Old\ Offering}$ = $100 – $60 = $40. Therefore, the break-even rate of cannibalization can be calculated as follows:

$$BER_{Cannibalization} = \frac{Margin_{New\ Offering}}{Margin_{Old\ Offering}} = \frac{\$10}{\$40} = 0.25$$

The break-even rate of cannibalization in this case is 0.25 or 25%, which means that to be profitable to the company, no more than 25% of the sales volume of the new offering should come from the current offering, which in turn implies that at least 75% of the sales volume should come at the expense of competitors' offerings and/or from increasing the overall size of the market.

APPENDIX F

RELEVANT FRAMEWORKS

Each problem that I solved became a rule
which served afterwards to solve other problems.
— René Descartes, French philosopher,
mathematician, and physicist

The frameworks outlined in this book—the G-STIC framework, the 5-C framework, the 3-V framework, and the marketing mix framework—reflect the process by which a company develops a marketing plan to launch and manage its offerings. In addition, there are several other frameworks frequently used in marketing analysis and planning: the SWOT framework, the five forces framework, the product–market growth framework, the 4-P framework, the product life cycle framework, the critical path method, the responsibility assignment matrix, and the Gantt matrix. These frameworks are outlined in the following sections.

The SWOT Framework

The SWOT framework is a relatively simple and intuitive approach for evaluating a company's overall business condition. As implied by its name, the SWOT framework entails four factors: the company's *strengths* and *weaknesses*, and the *opportunities* and *threats* presented to the company by the environment in which it operates. These four factors are organized in a 2×2 matrix based on whether they are internal or external to the company, and whether they are favorable or unfavorable from the company's standpoint (Figure 1).

Figure 1. The SWOT Framework

To illustrate, factors such as loyal customers, strong brand name(s), patents and trademarks, know-how, experienced personnel, and access to scarce resources are typically classified as strengths, whereas factors such as disloyal customers, weak brand name(s), and lack of technological expertise are viewed as weaknesses. Similarly, factors such as emergence of a new, underserved customer segment and a favorable economic environment are considered opportunities, whereas a new competitive entry, increased product commoditization, and increased buyer and supplier power are considered threats.

The SWOT framework can also be thought of as a 5-C framework in which the Five Cs are partitioned into favorable or unfavorable factors. Thus, the analysis of strengths and weaknesses focuses on the company, and the analysis of opportunities and threats focuses on the other four Cs describing the market in which the company operates — customers, collaborators, competitors, and context.

The Five Forces Framework

The Five Forces framework, advanced by Michael Porter, offers an industry-based analysis of the competition and is often used for strategic industry-level decisions such as evaluating the viability of entering (or exiting) a particular industry.[9] According to this framework, competitiveness within an industry is determined by five factors: the bargaining power of suppliers, the bargaining power of buyers, the threat of new entrants, the threat of substitutes, and rivalry among extant competitors (Figure 2). The joint impact of these five factors defines the competitive environment in which a firm operates. The greater the bargaining power of suppliers and buyers, the threat of new market entrants and substitute products, and the rivalry among existing competitors, the greater the competition within the industry.

Figure 2. The Five Forces of Competition

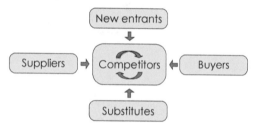

The Five Forces framework shares a number of similarities with the 5-C framework, as both frameworks aim to facilitate analysis of the market in which a company operates. At the same time, these frameworks differ in the way they define the market. The Five Forces framework takes an industry perspective to analyze the competition within the industry. In contrast, the 5-C framework is customer-centric rather than industry-focused, meaning that it defines the market based on customer needs rather than the industry in which the company competes. As a result, the 5-C framework defines competitors based on their ability to fulfill customer needs and create market value, and is not concerned with whether the company and its competitors operate within the bounds of the same industry.

The Product–Market Growth Framework

The Product–Market Growth framework (also referred to as the Ansoff matrix) offers a practical approach to evaluating market opportunities by linking customer segments to product development opportunities.[10] This framework is typically presented as a 2×2 matrix in which one of the factors represents the type of offering (current vs. new) and the other factor represents the type of customers (current vs. new). The resulting four product–market strategies are: *market penetration, market development, product development,* and *diversification* (Figure 3).

Figure 3. The Product–Market Growth Framework

	Current customers	New customers
Current products	Market penetration	Market development
New products	Product development	Diversification

- **Market penetration** aims to increase sales of an existing offering to a company's current customers. A common market-penetration strategy involves increasing the usage rate. To illustrate, airlines stimulate demand from current customers by adopting frequent-flyer programs, cereal manufacturers enclose repurchase coupons in their offerings, and orange juice producers promote drinking orange juice throughout the day rather than only for breakfast.

- **Market development** aims to grow sales by promoting an existing offering to new customers. Popular market-development strategies include price promotions (price reductions, coupons, and rebates), new distribution channels, and communication strategies focused on new customer segment(s).

- **Product development** aims to grow sales by developing new (to the company) offerings for existing customers. The two most common product-development strategies include developing entirely new offerings or extending the current product line by modifying existing offerings.

- **Diversification** aims to grow sales by introducing new offerings to new customers. Because both the offering and the customers are new to the company, this approach tends to be riskier than the other product-market growth strategies. The primary rationale for diversification is to take advantage of growth opportunities in areas in which the company has no presence.

The four strategies identified above are not mutually exclusive: A company can pursue multiple product-market growth strategies. However, companies using multiple growth strategies need to prioritize these strategies and focus on those that are most effective in enabling them to achieve their strategic goals.

The 4-P Framework

The 4-P framework identifies four key decisions that managers must make when designing and managing a given offering. These decisions involve the functionality and design of the company's *product*, the *price* at which the product is offered to target customers, the company's *promotion* of the product to target customers, and the retail outlets in which the company will *place* the product. The 4-P framework is intuitive and easy to remember, factors that have contributed to its popularity.

Despite its popularity, the 4-P framework has a number of limitations. One such limitation is that it does not distinguish between the product and service aspects of the offering. The fact that the 4-P framework does not explicitly account for the *service* element of the offering is a key drawback in today's service-oriented business environment, in which a growing number of companies are switching from a product-based to a service-based business model.

Another limitation of the 4-P framework is that the *brand* is not defined as a separate factor and instead is viewed as part of the product. The product and brand are different aspects of the offering and can exist independently of each other. An increasing number of companies including Lacoste, Disney, and Prada outsource their product manufacturing in order to focus their efforts on building and managing their brands.

The 4-P framework also comes up short in defining the term *promotion*. Promotion is a broad concept that includes two distinct types of activities: *incentives*—such as price promotions, coupons, and trade promotions—and *communication*, such as advertising, public relations, social media, and personal selling. Each of these two activities has a distinct role in the value-creation process. Incentives enhance the offering's value, whereas communication informs customers about the offering without necessarily enhancing its value. Using a single term to refer to these distinct activities muddles the unique role that they play in creating market value.

The limitations of the 4-P framework can be overcome by defining the market offering in terms of seven, rather than four, attributes—product, service, brand, price, incentives, communication, and distribution—as implied by the marketing mix framework discussed earlier in this chapter. The four Ps can be easily mapped onto the seven attributes defining the market offering, whereby the first P comprises product, service, and brand; price is the second P; incentives and communication are the third P; and distribution is the fourth P (Figure 4). The marketing mix framework outlined earlier in this chapter presents a more refined version of the 4-P framework that offers a more accurate and actionable approach to designing a company's offering.

Figure 4. The 4-P Framework

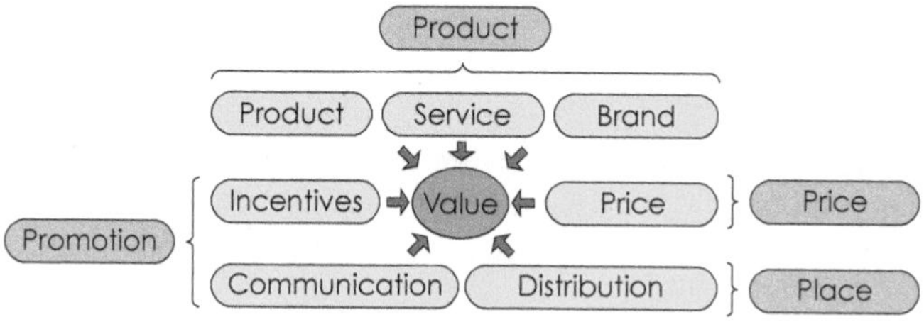

The Product Life Cycle Framework

The product life cycle framework describes the general trend of products and services as they progress through different stages in the marketplace. Life cycle can be defined in terms of a product category (e.g., mobile communication devices), a product class (e.g., smartphones), or a particular product (e.g., iPhone). The concept of a product life cycle is based on four key assumptions: (1) products have a limited life, (2) they pass through distinct stages, (3) their profitability depends on the stage, and, as a result, (4) different stages require different marketing strategies.

The product life cycle framework is based on the idea that products have a finite life in which they go through four distinct stages: introduction, growth, maturity, and decline.[11] During the *introduction* stage, product awareness is low and there are few competitors. As the product takes off during the *growth* stage, the number of competitors entering the market increases. At *maturity*, the number of competitors tends to peak, the market becomes saturated, and industry profitability starts to decline because of intensifying competition. Finally, the *decline* stage is characterized by falling demand for the product, relatively low profitability, and a decreasing number of competitors stemming from consolidation and exit from the market. The four stages of the product life cycle and the corresponding market conditions at each stage are illustrated in Figure 5.

Figure 5. The Product Life Cycle Framework

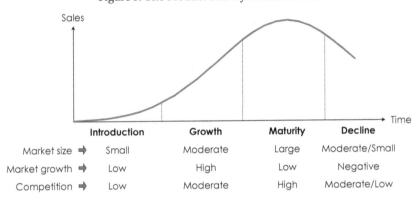

	Introduction	Growth	Maturity	Decline
Market size ➡	Small	Moderate	Large	Moderate/Small
Market growth ➡	Low	High	Low	Negative
Competition ➡	Low	Moderate	High	Moderate/Low

Offering strategies vary across a product's life cycle. At the introduction stage, companies typically offer a single product targeted to the most likely adopters. As the product enters the growth stage, the number of customers adopting the product increases, and so does the diversity of customers' needs. To address the diverse needs of its target customers, companies introduce product variants designed to better meet the needs of different customer segments. The number of product variants typically peaks at maturity and starts decreasing as the product enters the decline stage; profit margins shrink and companies focus on best-selling products, phasing out product variants with insufficient volume to meet their profit goals.

The stage of an offering's life cycle also influences the company's communication. In the early stages of a product category, communication aims primarily at creating awareness among early adopters. As the product category enters the growth stage, a company's communication goals shift to creating awareness of the product within the mass market while at the same time differentiating its offerings from those of competitors. As the product category matures and the majority of customers are aware of the category benefits, communication shifts from creating awareness of the category benefits to differentiating the company's offering by highlighting its benefits vis-à-vis the competition. This emphasis on product differentiation continues as the category enters its decline stage; however, at this point overall communication expenditures tend to decline.

The bell-shaped curve implied by the product life cycle framework is merely a stylized example of the product life cycle. In reality, many products and services follow different patterns that, for example, may include multiple peaks at different stages of the life cycle. In this context, the product life-cycle curve is primarily a descriptive tool used to illustrate the general trend of products as they go through different stages in the market. It is not designed to predict the future market success of a particular product or exactly when the product will reach the growth, maturity, and decline stages.

Critical Path Method

The Critical Path Method (CPM) is a mathematically derived algorithm for scheduling project activities. CPM is based on the notion that the implementation of a project is controlled by a relatively small set of activities that make up the path that takes the longest time to move through the activity network (i.e., the sequence of activities that adds up to the longest overall duration). The goal of CPM, therefore, is to identify these "critical" activities and use them as the backbone (often referred to as the critical path) of the project schedule. To this end, the CPM calculates the longest path of planned activities to the end of the project, as well as the earliest and latest that each activity can begin and end while keeping the project on schedule. The advantage of identifying these key activities is that it allows other, less crucial activities to be planned around the activities composing the critical path.

CPM typically involves six key steps: (1) identify the specific activities and milestones associated with the project, (2) determine the optimal sequence of individual activities (which activities must precede and which must follow others), (3) develop a diagram representing the individual activities and their relationship, (4) estimate the time and cost allocated to each activity, (5) determine the longest time path through the network (also referred to as the critical path), and (6) monitor the project implementation, modifying the diagram when necessary.

The process of identifying the critical path is illustrated in Figure 6. Here specific outcomes are depicted by circles and individual activities are depicted by arrows; the numbers associated with each arrow indicate the duration (e.g., in weeks) of the corresponding activity. Analysis of the relationship among the different outcomes indicates that Outcomes C and D need to be completed prior to achieving the desired Outcome E, Outcomes A and B need to be achieved prior to achieving Outcome C, and Outcome A needs to be achieved prior to achieving Outcome D. Analysis of the time necessary to complete each individual activity further indicates that the longest path through the network is A-C-E (12 weeks). Hence, A-C-E is the critical path that should be used as the backbone for scheduling the remaining activities.

Figure 6. The Critical Path Method

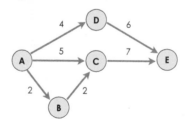

A potential limitation of the CPM model is its reliance on a manager's ability to estimate the interdependence and the relative completion time of the individual activities necessary for completing the project. This limitation of the CPM model is addressed in an alternative approach commonly referred to as Project Evaluation and Review Technique (PERT), which allows a range of durations to be specified for each activity. Thus, PERT is very similar to CPM in that both models employ the notion of critical path and involve the same six implementation steps. The key distinction between the two is the manner in which the duration of a given activity is estimated. Unlike CPM, which relies on a single duration estimate, PERT involves calculating a weighted average of three different estimates of the expected completion time (optimistic, most likely, and pessimistic). Recent extensions of PERT and CPM enable managers to control resources other than time and costs, making these models general enough to be applicable to most business implementation tasks.

Responsibility Assignment Matrix

The Responsibility Assignment Matrix (RAM) is a commonly used approach for linking business processes to the company's organizational infrastructure and assigning project-related activities to specific entities within the organization. RAM outlines the key components of a project and designates the functional role (e.g., project manager, product engineer, sales force manager) and/or the specific entity responsible for the implementation of each task. The matrix typically lists the key business tasks on the vertical axis and lists the corresponding roles on the horizontal axis (Figure 7). Each role can be performed either by an individual or a team, and each individual/team can play multiple roles.

Figure 7. The Responsibility Assignment Matrix

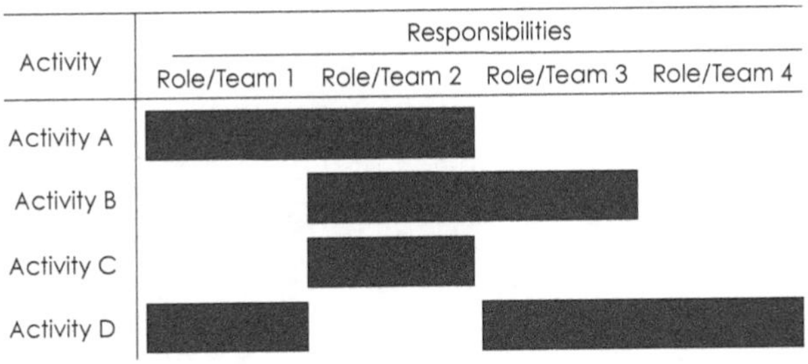

The Responsibility Assignment Matrix is sometimes referred to as RACI, an acronym for the key roles involved in action planning: responsible, accountable, consulted, and informed. Here, *responsible* refers to the entity responsible for completing the task (e.g., product engineer); *accountable* refers to the entity accountable for the accurate and timely completion of the task (e.g., project manager); *consulted* refers to entities that are provided with information about the project and engage in two-way communication (e.g., functional experts such as accounting, legal, IT departments); and *informed* refers to entities that are kept informed about progress only through one-way communication (e.g., cross-functional teams affected by the project outcome).

Gantt Matrix

The Gantt matrix maps the individual tasks and their timeline in a format that enables a manager to easily identify the optimal sequence and duration of these tasks in the context of the entire project. A popular method of representing the implementation plan, the Gantt matrix uses bars to visually represent the timeline and duration of each individual task. Named after Henry Gantt—an American mechanical engineer and management consultant—this chart typically indicates the start and the finish dates of the key project tasks (Figure 8).

Figure 8. Gantt Matrix

The typical Gantt matrix lists on the vertical axis all the tasks to be performed and lists on the horizontal axis a description of each task (e.g., task specifics, skill level needed to perform the task, and the individual/team assigned to the task); horizontal bars represent the starting time and duration of each task. Depending on the nature of the project, the time frame can be expressed in hours, days, weeks, months, or any other time units.

Essential Marketing Concepts

Above-the-Line Communications: Company communications are often divided into two categories: Above-the-Line (ATL) communications, which encompass mass media advertising such as television commercials, radio, and print advertisements; and Below-the-Line (BTL) communications, which include public relations, event sponsorship, personal selling, and direct mail. Historically, the term ATL was used in reference to communications for which an advertising agency charged a commission to place in mass media, whereas the term BTL was used in reference to communications that involved a standard charge rather than a commission. Currently, the terms ATL and BTL are used loosely to indicate an emphasis on mass media (ATL) versus one-on-one communications (BTL). The current use of BTL often includes customer and trade incentives as well.

Advertising Allowance: A form of trade promotion in which retailers are given a discount in exchange for advertising manufacturers' products.

Below-the-Line (BTL) Communications: See *above-the-line communication*.

Bonus Merchandise: Free goods offered as a reward for purchasing a particular item.

Brand Audit: A comprehensive analysis of a brand, most often to determine the sources of brand equity.

Brand Extension: The strategy of using the same brand name in a different context (e.g., different product category or different price tier). There are two main types of brand extensions: within-category extensions and cross-category extensions. In within-category brand extensions, the same brand name is applied to several products within the same product category. In contrast, in cross-category brand extensions, the same brand name is applied to products in different categories. To illustrate, extending the Starbucks name to different coffee flavors is a within-category brand extension, whereas extending it to ice cream is considered a cross-category brand extension.

Branded House: See *umbrella branding*.

Cannibalization: The scenario in which a newly introduced offering steals share from other offering(s) within the same company. In many cases, cannibalization can have an overall positive impact (e.g., when the margins of the new offering are higher than those of the cannibalized one, or when the new offering seeks to achieve different strategic goals).

Captive Pricing: See *complementary pricing*.

Carryover Effect in Advertising: Impact of an advertising campaign that extends beyond the time frame of the campaign. To illustrate, an advertising effort made in a given period might generate sales in subsequent periods.

Channel Conflict: The tension between members of a distribution channel (e.g., a manufacturer and a retailer), often caused by different profit optimization strategies of each channel member. See also *horizontal channel conflict* and *vertical channel conflict*.

Cobranding: Branding strategy that involves combining two or more brands. Examples of cobranding include United Airlines–JPMorgan Chase–Visa credit cards, Lexus "Coach edition" sport utility vehicles, and HP–iPod MP3 players.

Comparative Advertising: Advertising strategy whereby a given offering is directly compared with another offering.

Competitive Parity Budgeting: Budget allocation strategy based on (1) matching competitors' absolute level of spending or (2) the proportion per point of market share.

Complementary Pricing: Pricing strategy applicable to uniquely compatible, multipart offerings, whereby a company charges a relatively low introductory price for the first part of the offering and higher prices for the other parts. Classic examples include razors and blades, printers and cartridges, and cell phones and cell phone service.

Consumer Packaged Goods (CPG): A term used to describe consumer products packaged in portable containers: food, beverages, health and beauty aids, tobacco, and cleaning supplies.

Consumer Promotions: Promotional activities aimed at the consumer (rather than the retailer). Typical consumer promotional activities include free samples, coupons, rebates, and point-of-purchase displays.

Cooperative Advertising: Advertising strategy in which a manufacturer and a retailer jointly advertise their offering to consumers. In this case, the manufacturer pays a portion of a retailer's advertising costs in return for the retailer featuring its products, services, and brands.

Cooperative Advertising Allowance: An incentive paid by the manufacturer to a distributor in return for featuring its offerings in a retailer's advertisements. The magnitude of the allowance can be determined as a percentage of the distributor's advertising costs or as a fixed dollar amount per unit.

Cost-Plus Pricing: A pricing method in which the final price is determined by adding a fixed markup to the cost of the product. It is easy to calculate and is commonly used in industries where profit margins are relatively stable. Its key drawback is that it does not take into account customer demand and competitive pricing.

Cross-Price Elasticity: The percentage change in the quantity sold of a given offering caused by a percentage change in the price of another offering.

Deceptive Pricing: The practice of presenting an offering's price to the buyer in a way that is deliberately misleading. Deceptive pricing is illegal in the United States.

Demographics: A set of characteristics used to describe a given population. Demographics commonly used in marketing include factors such as population size and growth, age dispersion, geographic dispersion, ethnic background, income, mobility, education, employment, and household composition.

Detailers: Indirect sales force promoting pharmaceuticals to dentists, doctors, and pharmacists so that they, in turn, recommend the brand to the consumer.

Direct Channel: Distribution strategy in which the manufacturer and the end customer interact directly with each other without intermediaries.

Display Allowance: An incentive paid by the manufacturer to a distributor in return for the distributor prominently displaying its products and/or services.

Everyday Low Pricing (EDLP): A pricing strategy in which a retailer maintains low prices without frequent price promotions.

Experience Curve Pricing: A pricing strategy based on an anticipated future lower cost structure resulting from economies of scale and experience curve effects.

Fighting Brand: A downscale (lower priced) brand introduced to shield a major brand from low-priced competitors.

Forward Buying: Increasing the channel inventory, usually to take advantage of a manufacturer's promotion or in anticipation of price increases.

Go-to-Market Plan: A type of marketing plan, typically referring to a new product launch plan, focusing on the communication and distribution aspects of the marketing plan.

Grey Market: A market in which products are sold through unauthorized channels.

Heterogeneous Market: Market composed of customers who vary (i.e., are heterogeneous) in their response to a company's offering.

High-Low Pricing: Pricing strategy in which a retailer's prices fluctuate over time, typically a result of heavy reliance on sales promotions. See also *everyday low pricing*.

Homogeneous Market: Market composed of customers likely to react in a similar manner to the company's offering (e.g., they seek the same benefits, have similar financial resources, can be reached via the same means of communication, and have access to the offering through the same distribution channels).

Horizontal Channel Conflict: A conflict between members within the same level of the channel (e.g., between two retailers). Horizontal conflicts occur when different channels target the same customer segment with identical or substitutable offerings (e.g., different retailers selling the same product to the same customer).

Horizontal Differentiation: A product-line strategy in which offerings vary on benefits that do not imply a universal preference ordering. For example, offerings such as different types of soft drinks (regular, cherry, vanilla, diet, or caffeine-free), different yogurt flavors, and different product colors compose horizontally differentiated product lines. Note that although price may vary across horizontally differentiated offerings, it is not the key differentiating factor. See also *vertical differentiation*.

Horizontal Price Fixing: A practice in which competitors explicitly or implicitly collaborate to set prices. Price fixing is illegal in the United States.

House of Brands: Term used in reference to a branding strategy in which a company holds a portfolio of individual and typically unrelated brands. Companies using this strategy include Procter & Gamble, Unilever, and Diageo. See also *umbrella branding*.

Hybrid Channel: Distribution strategy in which the manufacturer and the end customer interact with each other through multiple channels (directly and through intermediaries).

Image Pricing: See *price signaling*.

Indirect Channel: Distribution strategy in which the manufacturer and the end customer interact with each other through intermediaries.

Ingredient Branding: A form of cobranding that involves ingredient branding in which an ingredient or component of a product has its own brand identity, such as Teflon surface protector, Gore-Tex fabrics, NutraSweet and Splenda sweeteners, and Intel microprocessors.

Institutional Advertising: Advertising strategy designed to build goodwill or an image for an organization (rather than to promote specific offerings).

Learning Curve: The curve describing how costs of production decline as cumulative output increases over time. The logic behind this concept is that labor hours per unit decline on repetitive tasks. The term learning curve is often used interchangeably with the concept of experience curve.

Loss Leader: Pricing strategy that involves setting a low price for an offering (often at or below cost) in an attempt to increase the sales of other products and services. For example, a retailer might set a low price for a popular item in an attempt to build store traffic, thus increasing the sales of other, more profitable items.

Market-Growth Strategy: A marketing strategy aimed at attracting new users to the category (as opposed to selectively targeting current category users). Because of its focus on increasing the overall category demand, the market-growth strategy is sometimes referred to as primary demand stimulation. See also *steal-share strategy*.

Merchandisers: Indirect sales force that offers support to retailers for in-store activities such as shelf location, pricing, and compliance with special programs.

Niche Strategy: Marketing strategy aimed at a distinct and relatively small customer segment.

Occasion-Based Targeting: Targeting strategy that groups customers based on purchase and consumption occasions. Occasion-based targeting is useful in cases in which customer needs vary across purchase occasions, and the same customer is likely to fall into different usage-based segments at different times. For example, when buying wine, a customer's preference might vary as a function of the occasion (for cooking, for daily consumption, for a special occasion, or for a gift). By focusing on usage occasions rather than on the individual characteristics of the customer, occasion-based targeting accounts for the fact that the same customer is likely to display different needs depending on the occasion. Unlike user-based targeting, which assumes that customer needs do not vary across purchase occasions, occasion-based targeting does not make such an assumption, implying that an individual customer (or segment) can have different needs on different purchase occasions.

Off-Invoice Incentive: Any temporary price discounts offered by manufacturers to distributors.

Penetration Pricing: A pricing strategy aimed at rapidly gaining market share. This strategy often leads to higher sales volume, albeit at lower margins.

Performance Gap: A discrepancy between the desired and the actual state of affairs, between the goal and the reality. Performance gaps often include discrepancies between desired and actual gross and net revenues, profit margins, and market share.

Point-of-Purchase Advertising: The promotional materials displayed at the point of purchase (e.g., in a retail store).

Predatory Pricing: A strategy that involves selling below cost with the intent of driving competitors out of business. Predatory pricing is illegal in the United States.

Prestige Pricing: Pricing strategy whereby the price is set at a relatively high level for the purpose of creating an exclusive image of the offering.

Price Discrimination: A strategy that involves charging different buyers different prices for goods of equal grade and quality.

Price Fixing: A practice in which companies conspire to set prices for a given product or service. Price fixing is illegal in the United States.

Price Segmentation: See *price discrimination.*

Price Signaling: (1) Pricing strategy that aims to capitalize on price–quality inferences (higher priced products are also likely to be higher quality), primarily used when the actual product benefits are not readily observable (also known as prestige pricing); (2) Indirect communication (direct price collusion is prohibited by law) between companies aimed at indicating their intentions with respect to their pricing strategy.

Price Skimming: A pricing strategy in which a firm sets a high initial price to maximize profit margins, usually at the expense of market share.

Private Label: Branding strategy in which an offering is branded by the retailer (Kirkland Signature, Costco's private brand; Kenmore, Sears' brand for home appliances; White Cloud, Walmart's private label for laundry detergents). Private labels (also referred to as store brands) are often contrasted with national brands, which are branded by the manufacturer or a third party (e.g., Coca-Cola, GE, and Nike) rather than by the retailer. Typically, private labels tend to be less expensive than national brands, although there are many exceptions, such as private labels offered by upscale retailers (Nordstrom, Marks & Spencer).

Product-Line Pricing: Pricing strategy in which the price of each individual offering is determined as a function of the offering's place in the relevant product line.

Psychographics: Relatively stable individual characteristics such as personality, moral values, attitudes, interests, and lifestyle.

Public Service Announcement (PSA): Nonprofit advertising that uses free space or time donated by the media.

Push and Pull Strategies: Promotion strategies depicting the flow of promotions (incentives and communication) from the manufacturer to target customers. *Pull strategy* refers to the practice of creating demand for a company's offering by promoting the offering directly to end users, who in turn demand the offering from intermediaries, ultimately "pulling" the offering through the channel (Figure 1). To illustrate, the manufacturer may extensively advertise its products and services to end users and/or promote its offerings using means such as direct mail, coupons, contests, etc. In contrast, *push strategy* refers to the practice of creating demand for a company's offering by incentivizing channel members, who in turn push the product downstream to end users. For example, the manufacturer may offer high margins on its products and services so that retailers have a vested interest in selling them. The manufacturer may also educate a retailer's sales force about the benefits of its offerings and provide the retailer with promotional materials, thus facilitating the sales process.

Figure 1. Push and Pull Promotions

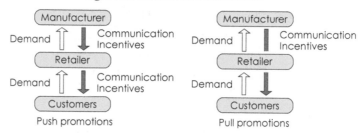

Reminder Advertising: Advertising strategy designed to maintain awareness and stimulate repurchase of an already established offering.

Repositioning: A change in the positioning of a given offering.

Reverse Logistics: The process of reclaiming recyclable and reusable materials and returns for repair, remanufacturing, or disposal.

Run-of-Press Coupons: The coupons that appear in the actual pages of a newspaper (rather than inserted as a separate page). Sometimes run-of-press coupons are part of an advertisement promoting the same offering.

Shrinkage: A term used by retailers to describe theft of goods by customers and employees.

Slotting Allowance: An incentive paid to a distributor to allocate shelf space for a new product.

Spiffs: Incentives such as cash premiums, prizes, or additional commissions given directly to the salesperson (rather than the distributor) as a reward for selling a particular item. Because they encourage the retailer's sales personnel to "push" the product to customers, spiffs are often referred to as "push money."

Steal-Share Strategy: A marketing strategy referring to a company's activities aimed at attracting its competitors' customers rather than increasing the size of the entire market. Because of its focus on attracting only those customers who are already using competitors' products, the steal-share strategy is also referred to as selective demand stimulation. See also *market-growth strategy*.

Stock Keeping Unit (SKU): A unique identifier assigned to each distinct product or service.

Stocking Allowance: An incentive paid to a distributor to carry extra inventory in anticipation of an increase in demand.

Store Brand: See *private label*.

Strategic Business Unit (SBU): An operating company unit with a discrete set of offerings sold to an identifiable group of customers, in competition with a well-defined set of competitors.

Sub-Brand: A second-tier brand name often used to mitigate the potential drawbacks of a direct brand extension, while leveraging the core brand to support the extension (e.g., Courtyard by Marriott, Ford Mustang, and Porsche Cayenne).

Teaser Advertising: Communication strategy designed to create interest in an offering while providing little or no information about it.

Trade Allowance: A broad range of trade incentives (e.g., slotting allowance, stocking allowance, and advertising allowance) offered as a reward for conducting promotional activities on behalf of the manufacturer. Trade allowances are typically implemented as a discount from the wholesale price rather than as a separate promotional payment. From an accounting standpoint, they are often considered as a discount to the channel rather than as a separate marketing expense.

Trademark: A distinctive sign that identifies certain goods or services as those produced or provided by a specific entity.

Two-Part Pricing: See *complementary pricing*.

Umbrella Branding (also referred to as branded-house strategy): A branding strategy that involves using a single brand for all of a company's products. For example, General Electric, Heinz, and Virgin use a single brand for nearly all of their products.

User-Based Targeting: Targeting strategy that groups customers based on their relatively stable individual characteristics, which are likely to determine their needs and behavior across different purchase and consumption occasions. User-based targeting focuses on individual customers, assuming that their preferences are constant across usage occasions, whereas occasion-based targeting focuses on usage occasions rather than on individual customers. User-based targeting assumes that customer needs do not vary across purchase occasions, and, hence, that an individual's needs can be fulfilled with a single offering. Accordingly, user-based targeting is appropriate in settings in which customers' needs are relatively stable and can be used as a reliable predictor of their behavior on any particular purchase occasion. To illustrate, the preference for regular versus light (diet) soft drinks is fairly stable across individuals and calls for user-based targeting. User-based targeting can be viewed as a special case (assuming that customer preferences are constant across usage occasions) of the more general approach of need-based targeting.

Vertical Channel Conflict: A conflict that occurs between different levels of the same channel (e.g., manufacturer–retailer) and is often caused by differences in their profit optimization strategies.

Vertical Differentiation: A product-line strategy in which offerings can be easily ordered in terms of the relative attractiveness of their benefits and costs, such that this preference ordering is the same for all target customers. To illustrate, most Marriott customers will rate Ritz-Carlton hotels as superior to Marriott hotels, which in turn are likely to be rated superior to Courtyard by Marriott hotels. Because better performance typically comes at a higher price, vertically differentiated products and services typically belong to different price tiers (hence the name vertical differentiation).

Volume Discount: Price reductions based on purchase volume.

Volume Rebate (Volume Bonus): An incentive paid by the manufacturer to a distributor as a reward for achieving certain purchase-volume benchmarks (e.g., selling 1,000 units per quarter).

Wearout: A decrease in the effectiveness of a communication campaign from decreased consumer interest in the message, often resulting from repetition.

Yield-Management Pricing: Pricing strategy whereby the price is set to maximize revenue for a fixed capacity within a given time frame (frequently used by airlines and hotels).

Notes

1 For more detailed discussion of marketing strategy and tactics see Chernev, Alexander (2018), *Strategic Marketing Management* (9th ed.). Chicago, IL: Cerebellum Press.

2 The view of customer value creation as a process of managing attractiveness, awareness, and availability is a streamlined version of the 4-A framework that delineates acceptability, affordability, accessibility, and awareness as the key sources of customer value. See Sheth, Jagdish and Rajendra Sisodia (2012). *The 4 A's of Marketing: Creating Value for Customer, Company and Society*. New York, NY: Routledge.

3 This sample marketing plan was developed solely for the purposes of this book. Some of the information contained in this document has been modified to better illustrate specific aspects of writing a marketing plan. This document should not be used as a primary source of information either for Align Technology or for its offerings. This marketing plan is largely based on the S-1 registration statement for the initial public offering of Align Technology Inc., as filed with the Securities and Exchange Commission on November 14, 2000. Some of the information in Section 2.2 is based on *Invisalign: Orthodontics Unwired* (2004) by Anne Coughlan and Julie Hennessy, Kellogg School of Management, Northwestern University.

4 This sample marketing plan was developed solely for the purposes of this book. Some of the information contained in this document has been modified to better illustrate specific aspects of writing a marketing plan. This document should not be used as a primary source of information either for Align Technology or for its offerings. This marketing plan is largely based on the 10-K reports (annual reports) filed by Align Technology Inc. with the Securities and Exchange Commission in 2008, 2009, and 2010.

5 A detailed analysis of DeWalt's strategy and tactics is offered in Chernev, Alexander (2018), *Strategic Marketing Management* (9th ed.). Chicago, IL: Cerebellum Press.

6 This sample marketing plan was developed solely for the purposes of this book. Some of the information contained in this document has been modified to better illustrate specific aspects of writing a marketing plan. This document should not be used as a primary source of information either for Black & Decker or for its offerings. The reported data are based on "The Black & Decker Corporation (A): Power Tools Division" (595-057), "The Black & Decker Corporation (B): "Operation Sudden Impact" (595-060), "The Black & Decker Corporation (B): 'Operation Sudden Impact'" (596-510), and "The Black & Decker Corporation (C): Operation Sudden Impact Results, 1992-1994" (595-061), Harvard Business School: Harvard Business School Publishing, Boston, MA.

7 The examples used in this chapter are for illustration purposes only and might not adequately reflect the companies' actual positioning strategies.

8 Reichheld, Fred (2003), "The One Number You Need to Grow," *Harvard Business Review*, 81 (December), 1–11.

9 Porter, Michael E. (1979), "How Competitive Forces Shape Strategy," *Harvard Business Review*, 57 (March–April), 137–145.

10 Ansoff, H. Igor (1979), *Strategic Management*. New York, NY: John Wiley & Sons.

11 Levitt, Theodore (1965), "Exploit the Product Life Cycle," *Harvard Business Review*, 43, (November–December), 81–94.

CPSIA information can be obtained
at www.ICGtesting.com
Printed in the USA
LVHW060902301218
602197LV00002B/34/P

9 781936 572557

"Alexander Chernev has written the clearest handbook that I have seen on how to write a marketing plan, cover all the bases, and yet keep it short. His two example marketing plans, one for a new product launch and the second for an existing product, breathe life into the planning concepts."

Philip Kotler

S.C. Johnson & Son Distinguished Professor of Marketing, Kellogg School of Management, Northwestern University and one of the world's foremost marketing experts

"Alexander Chernev's *The Marketing Plan Handbook* can help any marketer achieve the skill to design creative, effective, efficient marketing plans. It offers clear, concise insights and guidelines for designing marketing plans that will truly work."

Kevin Lane Keller

E.B. Osborn Professor of Marketing at the Tuck School of Business, Dartmouth College and author of *Strategic Brand Management* — the leading branding textbook

"An excellent book offering a streamlined, no-nonsense roadmap to writing impactful marketing plans."

Jean-Claude Larreche

The Alfred Heineken Chaired Professor of Marketing at INSEAD, creator of Markstrat — the leading strategic marketing simulation — and author of *The Momentum Effect*

"If you are going to write a marketing plan, you need to start with Chernev's *The Marketing Plan Handbook*. And, of course, every business needs to have a marketing plan."

David Reibstein

William Stewart Woodside Professor of Marketing at the Wharton School, University of Pennsylvania and author of *Marketing Metrics: 50+ Metrics Every Manager Should Master*

ISBN 978-1-936572-55-7

90000

9 781936 572557

T2-FBO-084